D1123991

How to Use This Book

Look for these special features in this book:

SIDEBARS, **CHARTS**, **GRAPHS**, and original **MAPS** expand your understanding of what's being discussed—and also make useful sources for classroom reports.

FAQs answer common **F**requently **A**sked **Q**uestions about people, places, and things.

WOW FACTORS offer "Who knew?" facts to keep you thinking.

TRAVEL GUIDE gives you tips on exploring the state—either in person or right from your chair!

PROJECT ROOM provides fun ideas for school assignments and incredible research projects. Plus, there's a guide to primary sources—what they are and how to cite them.

Please note: All statistics are as up-to-date as possible at the time of publication. Population data is taken from the 2010 census.

Consultants: Linda C. Ivany, Associate Professor of Earth Sciences, Syracuse University; William Loren Katz; Jennifer Murphy, Albany Public Library; Garet D. Livermore, New York State Historical Association

Book production by The Design Lab

Library of Congress Cataloging-in-Publication Data
Somervill, Barbara A.
 New York / by Barbara A. Somervill. — Revised edition.
  pages cm. — (America, the beautiful. Third series)
 Includes bibliographical references and index.
 ISBN 978-0-531-24895-9 (lib. bdg.)
 1. New York (State)—Juvenile literature. I. Title.
 F119.3.S66 2014
 974.7—dc23   2013032830

No part of this publication may be reproduced in whole or in part, or stored in a retrieval system, or transmitted in any form or by any means, electronic, mechanical, photocopying, recording, or otherwise, without written permission of the publisher. For information regarding permission, write to Scholastic Inc., 557 Broadway, New York, NY 10012.

©2014, 2008 Scholastic Inc.
All rights reserved. Published in 2014 by Children's Press, an imprint of Scholastic Inc.
Printed in the United States of America 141
SCHOLASTIC, CHILDREN'S PRESS, and associated logos are trademarks and/or registered trademarks of Scholastic Inc.

1 2 3 4 5 6 7 8 9 10 R 23 22 21 20 19 18 17 16 15 14

New York

BY BARBARA A. SOMERVILL

Third Series, Revised Edition

Children's Press®
An Imprint of Scholastic Inc.
New York ★ Toronto ★ London ★ Auckland ★ Sydney
Mexico City ★ New Delhi ★ Hong Kong
Danbury, Connecticut

CONTENTS

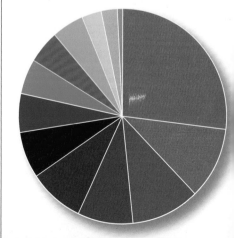

GROWTH AND CHANGE

PROSPECTUS
FOR AN ANTI-SLAVERY PAPER, TO BE ENTITLED
NORTH STAR.
FREDERICK DOUGLASS
Proposes to publish, in ROCHESTER, N. Y., a WEEKLY ANTI-SLAVERY PAPER, with the above title.
The object of the NORTH STAR will be to attack SLAVERY in all its forms and aspects; advocate UNIVERSAL EMANCIPATION; exalt the standard of PUBLIC MORALITY; promote the Moral and Intellectual Improvement of the COLORED PEOPLE; and hasten the day of FREEDOM to the Three Millions of our ENSLAVED FELLOW COUNTRYMEN.

MORE MODERN TIMES

TRAVEL GUIDE

PROJECT ROOM

★

CANADA

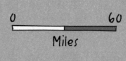
0   60
Miles

St. Lawrence

PLATTSBURGH

Lake Champlain

Six Nations
Indian Museum

Mount Marcy

CANADA

Adirondack
State Park
and Forest
Preserve

Hudson

VERMONT

NEW
HAMPS

LAKE ONTARIO

Oneida Lake

National
Baseball
Hall of Fame

New York State
Capitol Building

ROCHESTER

Erie Canal

Finger   Lakes

SYRACUSE

NEW
YORK

COOPERSTOWN

Valley

BUFFALO

ALBANY

Hudson

MASSACHUSETT

LAKE
ERIE

Niagara Falls

Finger Lakes
Region

Susquehanna

Catskills

Hudson

CONNECTICUT

Delaware

Solomon R.
Guggenheim
Museum

Bronx Zoo

Long Island

PENNSYLVANIA

BROADWAY
49

Broadway
Theatre
District

NEW YORK

Long
Island
Montau
Point

Statue of
Liberty

Empire
State
Building

ATLANTIC
OCEAN

QUICK FACTS

State capital: Albany
Largest city: New York City
Total area: 54,556 square miles
(141,300 sq km)
Highest point: Mount Marcy,
5,344 feet (1,629 m)
Lowest point: Sea level at the
Atlantic Ocean

MARYLAND

NEW
JERSEY

DEL.

Welcome to New York!

HOW DID NEW YORK GET ITS NAME?

In 1664, King Charles II of England gave his brother James, Duke of York, a gift—the Dutch colony of New Netherland. The king sent four ships, carrying 450 men, to the city of New Amsterdam and forced the Dutch military director-general, Peter Stuyvesant, to surrender both the city and the colony. New Netherland and New Amsterdam were renamed New York after the Duke of York. The New York of that time also included parts of present-day Connecticut, Delaware, and New Jersey. That's some gift!

NEW YORK

8

READ ABOUT

New York City's
Central Park
in autumn

CHAPTER ONE

LAND

★

NEW YORK IS A MEDIUM-SIZED STATE WITH A GIANT-SIZED REPUTATION. It may be best known for its big city, but did you know that New York is also a place of stunning scenery and vast wilderness? New York has glaciers to thank for its magnificent landscape. Over thousands of years, the advancing and retreating ice sheets covered nearly all of New York's 54,556 square miles (141,300 square kilometers), rounding off mountains, carving deep valleys and gorges, and creating spectacular waterfalls and sparkling lakes. From Mt. Marcy, its highest point at 5,344 feet (1,629 meters), to sea level along the Atlantic Ocean beaches of Long Island, New York is an amazing place.

Niagara Falls serves as a breathtaking natural border between New York and Canada.

LAND REGIONS

New York borders five states, several large bodies of water, and one other country. To the south and west lie New Jersey and Pennsylvania. From the western border, heading north, the state touches Lake Erie, Niagara Falls, Lake Ontario, and the St. Lawrence River. Rouses Point, near Lake Champlain, marks the northern boundary between New York, Vermont, and Canada. New York and Vermont share Lake Champlain. To the east, New York borders Massachusetts and Connecticut. At the state's southern extreme, Long Island stretches eastward from New York City. Long Island's south shore sits on the Atlantic Ocean, and its north shore on Long Island Sound. From north to south, New York has eight distinct geographic regions.

St. Lawrence Lowland

This nearly flat, gently rolling region lies along the northernmost reaches of the state and borders the St. Lawrence River. The area is known for its many dairy farms, as well as sand and gravel, crushed stone, and talc mining. New York's Thousand Islands are at the westernmost edge of the St. Lawrence Lowland.

The Adirondack Upland

This circular region lies southeast of the St. Lawrence Lowland. Lake Placid, Saranac Lake, and Tupper Lake are major bodies of water in the Adirondack Mountains, along with Lake Tear of the Clouds, the source spring of the Hudson River.

This region covers 5.7 million acres (2.3 million hectares) in northern New York. It is bounded to the east by Lake Champlain, to the south by the Mohawk River valley, to the west by the Black River, and to the north by the St. Lawrence River. The heavily forested region contains more than 2,200 lakes and 2,000 peaks, including Mount Marcy at 5,344 feet (1,629 m), the highest point in New York State. Its remote wilderness areas are among the most primitive in the eastern United States.

The Adirondack Mountains belong to the Canadian Shield, also known as the Laurentian Shield. They are

New York Geo-Facts

Along with the state's geographical highlights, this chart ranks New York's land, water, and total area compared to all other states.

Total area; rank	54,556 square miles (141,300 sq km); 27th
Land; rank	47,214 square miles (122,284 sq km); 30th
Water; rank	7,342 square miles (19,016 sq km); 7th
Inland water; rank	1,895 square miles (4,908 sq km); 10th
Coastal water; rank	981 square miles (2,541 sq km); 7th
Great Lakes; rank	3,988 square miles (10,329 sq km); 3rd
Territorial water; rank	479 square miles (1,241 sq km); 14th
Geographic center	Madison County, 12 miles (19 km) south of Oneida and 26 miles (42 km) southwest of Utica
Latitude	40° 29' 40" N to 45° 0' 42" N
Longitude	71° 47' 25" W to 79° 45' 54" W
Highest point	Mount Marcy, 5,344 feet (1,629 m)
Lowest point	Sea level at the Atlantic Ocean
Largest city	New York City
Longest river	Hudson River, 306 miles (492 km)

Source: U.S. Census Bureau, 2010 census

 The state of Rhode Island would fit inside New York more than 35 times.

THE STATE GEMSTONE: THE GARNET

One of the world's largest garnet mines is located on Gore Mountain in the Adirondacks. Although most people consider garnet a gem, it is a mineral that is widely used as an industrial abrasive. The name *garnet* comes from the Latin word for pomegranate, *malum granatum,* because the color of some garnets matched the red of pomegranate seeds. Garnet was adopted as New York's state gem in 1969.

Hikers can enjoy the magnificent views of Adirondack State Park and Preserve. At 6.1 million acres (2.5 million ha), it is the largest state park in the United States.

the only mountains in the eastern United States that aren't geologically part of the Appalachian chain. While the mountains themselves are relatively new, the rocks beneath them are some of the oldest on the planet.

Within the region is the Adirondack Forest Preserve, a 2.6-million-acre (1.1-million-ha) wilderness region that makes up about 40 percent of the larger Adirondack State Park and Preserve. The preserve was founded in 1885 and is protected by the New York State constitution as "forever wild." Adirondack State Park and Preserve was established in 1892, and although it is a state park, thousands of people live within its borders.

Tug Hill Plateau

West of the Adirondacks is the snowiest place east of the Rocky Mountains. It's the Tug Hill Plateau, a raised region where annual snowfall comes down in feet rather than inches.

New York Topography

Use the color-coded elevation chart to see on the map New York's high points (dark red to orange) and low points (green to dark green). Elevation is measured as the distance above or below sea level.

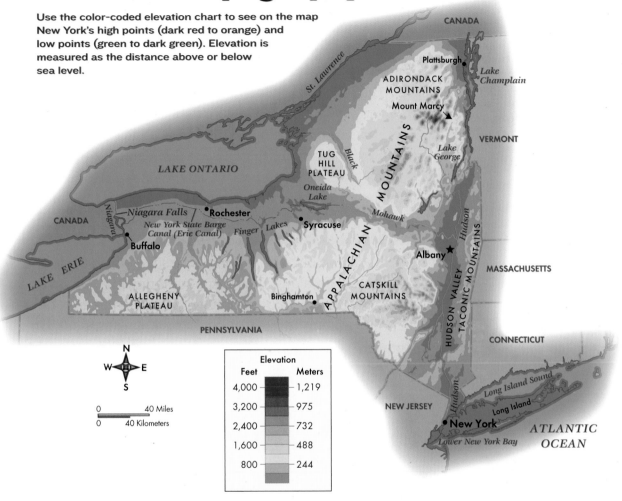

The Erie-Ontario Lowland

Just below Lake Erie and Lake Ontario, the Erie-Ontario Lowland is filled with rolling hills and highly productive farmland. Niagara Falls, a popular tourist attraction, lies on the border between New York and Canada.

The Appalachian Plateau

Directly to the south of the Erie-Ontario Lowland is the Appalachian Plateau. Also called the Allegheny Plateau,

New York's tallest waterfall is not Niagara Falls, but Inspiration Falls in Letchworth State Park. Inspiration Falls has a 350-foot (107-m) drop that flows only after a heavy rainfall.

This is Hammondsport in the Finger Lakes. Millions of hikers, campers, and water-sports enthusiasts visit this area each year.

this area features some of the most stunning scenery in the state. It is part of the Appalachian Mountain range that extends all the way from Alabama to Maine.

The Finger Lakes

The 11 Finger Lakes in central New York were carved into the Appalachian Plateau thousands of years ago by ice sheets expanding south from Canada. From east to west the lakes are the Otisco, Skaneateles, Owasco, Cayuga, Seneca, Keuka, Canandaigua, Honeoye, Canadice, Hemlock, and Conesus.

The Hudson-Mohawk Lowlands

The Hudson-Mohawk Lowlands spread out in an upside-down L shape along the west-to-east-flowing Mohawk River and the north-to-south flowing Hudson River. The Shawangunk Mountains, a low-lying range, border the Hudson River.

East of the Hudson River, a thin strip of the Taconic Mountains runs along New York's eastern border, shared with Massachusetts and Connecticut. One of the more interesting features of the Taconics is Stark's Knob, a mass of volcanic rock.

The Atlantic Coastal Plain

The southernmost portion of New York is part of the Atlantic Coastal Plain. All of Long Island is in the plain region. Along the southeastern shore, the island's beaches are stretches of sand with shifting dunes. Along the north shore, beaches are covered with tiny pebbles. Huge boulders stick out of Long Island Sound. These are remnants of the ice age, when a receding glacier dumped boulders called erratics.

RIVERS AND LAKES

New York abounds with lakes, ponds, rivers, and natural reservoirs. Lake Erie and Lake Ontario form part of New York's border with Canada. Water from Lake Erie pours over Niagara Falls toward Lake Ontario, which lies in lower altitude than Erie. Niagara Falls is actually three separate waterfalls (American, Bridal Veil, and Horseshoe) stretching between Canada and New York along the Niagara River.

On the northeastern side of the state, Lake Champlain and Lake George are two of the state's 6,713 natural lakes, ponds, and reservoirs. The largest lake completely within New York's borders is Oneida Lake, roughly 22 miles (35 kilometers) long and 5 miles (8 km) wide.

Lake Placid, with an average depth of about 50 feet (15 m), and Saranac Lake lie miles away from the Finger Lakes, high in the Adirondacks.

Throughout history, the Hudson River has been a major mode of transportation and shipping for the state's thriving economy.

New York's longest river is the Hudson, flowing south from Lake Tear of the Clouds to the Atlantic Ocean. The Hudson is 306 miles (492 km) long and discharges 21,400 cubic feet (606 cubic meters) of water per second into Lower New York Bay. The Mohawk River, 149 miles (238 km) long, is the Hudson's largest tributary. Along the state's northern border, the St. Lawrence River serves as a major waterway connecting the Great Lakes to the Atlantic. The Susquehanna River runs through New York, Pennsylvania, and Maryland. Its total length of 464 miles (747 km) makes it the longest river on the East Coast that drains into the Atlantic Ocean. The Genesee River runs 157 miles (253 km) through New York and Pennsylvania. It provides hydroelectric power for parts of Rochester.

CLIMATE

New York's climate is classified as a humid continental. The state experiences extremely cold winters, with 30 New York communities falling to record low temperatures below –40 degrees Fahrenheit (–40 degrees Celsius) over the past century. Northern New York shivers 35 to 45 days per year with below 0°F (–18°C) temperatures.

On summer days from May through September, temperatures often hit 90°F (32°C). In general, temperatures in the Adirondacks tend to be 10 to 15 degrees lower than temperatures in New York City.

On average, New York receives 40 inches (102 centimeters) of **precipitation** annually. The Tug Hill region gets 50 inches (127 cm) per year, while the area next to Lake Ontario averages only 30 inches (76 cm) yearly.

Not all of this precipitation comes in the form of rain. In upper New York State, snow can fall waist-deep in one storm. Drifts taller than an adult man are common. Blizzards occur most years, with 60 percent of the state receiving more than 70 inches (178 cm) yearly. In the Tug Hill region, called the snowbelt, residents can expect 175 inches (445 cm) of snow, while New York City dwellers usually only see 25 inches (64 cm) of snow. In February 2010, New York City dug its way out of 21 inches after a two-day snowfall, the fourth largest amount in the city's history. The record snowfall in New York City occurred in February 2006, when nearly 27 (69 cm) inches fell. All airports closed, and areas of Manhattan, Brooklyn, and Westchester experienced the rare phenomenon of thundersnow—peals of thunder during a snowstorm.

PLANT LIFE

Woodlands make up more than half of the state. There are some 150 kinds of trees, including the tulip tree, sweet gum, beech, sugar maple, ash, basswood, cherry, birch, red maple, and various oaks. There are a few cone-bearing trees as well, such as white pine and hemlock.

Weather Report

This chart shows record temperatures (high and low) for the state, as well as average temperatures (July and January) and average annual precipitation for New York City.

Record high temperature . . . . 108°F (42°C) at Troy on July 22, 1926
Record low temperature . . . −52°F (−47°C) at Old Forge on February 18, 1979
Average July temperature, New York City . . . . 77°F (25°C)
Average January temperature, New York City . . . . 33°F (−1°C)
Average annual precipitation, New York City . . . . . 45 inches (114 cm)

Source: National Climatic Data Center, NESDIS, NOAA, U.S. Department of Commerce

WORD TO KNOW

precipitation *all water that falls to earth, including rain, sleet, hail, snow, dew, fog, or mist*

FAQ

Q8 HOW CAN TUG HILL HAVE 50 INCHES OF PRECIPITATION, BUT 175 INCHES OF SNOW?

A8 Precipitation is all the forms of water that fall to the earth's surface, such as rain, sleet, snow, or hail. Snow, measured in inches or centimeters, contains both water and air. Ten inches (25 cm) of snow equals 1 inch (2.54 cm) of water. Tug Hill's annual 175 inches (445 cm) of snow equals only 17.5 inches (44 cm) of water.

In the Adirondacks, you will find heavily forested mountains rich with birch, pine, and balsam trees. And in the fall, the changing leaves are spectacular. During spring and summer, wildflowers cover the hillsides.

In the Appalachian Plateau, in the Finger Lakes region, vineyards produce an abundance of grapes for eating and wine making.

New York National Park Areas

This map shows some of New York's national parks, monuments, preserves, and other areas protected by the National Park Service.

CANADA

Plattsburgh

Lake Champlain

ADIRONDACK MOUNTAINS

Lake Placid

Adirondack State Park and Preserve

VERMONT

Adirondack

St. Lawrence

LAKE ONTARIO

CANADA

Niagara Falls • Rochester

Buffalo

Fort Stanwix NM

Syracuse

Saratoga NHP

Hudson

Women's Rights NHP

North Country NST

Theodore Roosevelt Inaugural NHS

LAKE ERIE

Albany ★

Martin Van Buren NHS

MASSACHUSETTS

Catskill Park

Vanderbilt Mansion NHS

PENNSYLVANIA

Upper Delaware SRR

CONNECTICUT

Home of Franklin D. Roosevelt NHS

Eleanor Roosevelt NHS

Appalachian NST

National Park units in the New York area:
African Burial Grounds NM
Castle Clinton NM
Ellis Island NM
Federal Hall NMEM
Gateway NRA
General Grant NMEM
Governors Island NM
Hamilton Grange NMEM
Lower East Side Tenement Museum NHS
Saint Paul's Church NHS
Statue of Liberty NM
Theodore Roosevelt Birthplace NHS

NEW JERSEY

Hudson

Sagamore Hill NHS

New York

Fire Island NS

ATLANTIC OCEAN

	National Park area
	State Park area
NHP	National Historic Park
NHS	National Historic Site
NMEM	National Memorial
NM	National Monument
NRA	National Recreation Area
NST	National Scenic Trail
NS	National Seashore
SRR	Scenic and Recreational River

N
W   E
S

0   40 Miles
0   40 Kilometers

ANIMAL LIFE

New York is home to many small mammals, such as the deer mouse, eastern cottontail, snowshoe hare, woodchuck, gray squirrel, muskrat, and raccoon. Larger mammals include the black bear, white-tailed deer, coyote, and beaver. In the Adirondacks, you'll find moose, particularly around the region's lakes. Some native birds include the eastern meadowlark, American goldfinch, cardinal, eastern bluebird, cedar waxwing, bluejay, red-tailed hawk, and various kinds of woodpeckers and owls.

ENVIRONMENTAL ISSUES

New York faces a number of environmental issues. They are handled through the New York State Department of Environmental Conservation (DEC). The DEC monitors environmental problems; manages hunting, fishing, and trapping licenses; and regulates the use of the state's natural resources. There are programs in place for cleaning up oil or chemical spills, clearing and handling **hazardous waste**, and ensuring the recovery of endangered and threatened plants and animals.

One of the greatest threats to New York's environment is **acid rain**. Acid rain contains chemicals that are released into the air through factory and automobile emissions. The chemicals fall back to earth with rain, snow, sleet, or hail. Acid rain reduces the amount of plant life in a region, which affects the animals that would normally feed on those plants. Acid rain falls into lakes and streams, killing **algae** and other small water creatures that keep lakes and streams healthy.

New York is a stunning collection of natural wonders. The state's government and people are committed to protecting their rivers, forests, and wildlife.

ENDANGERED ANIMALS

Have you ever seen a Karner blue butterfly or an Indiana bat? These are just two kinds of endangered animals that live in New York. Animals that are categorized as endangered are in jeopardy of dying out. New Yorkers are trying to protect these animals and preserve their environments. Other endangered animals in the state are the piping plover, the leatherback sea turtle, and the humpback whale.

WORDS TO KNOW

hazardous waste *chemical materials that are harmful to the environment*

acid rain *pollution that falls to the earth in the form of rain*

algae *plant or plantlike organisms that live in water*

White-tailed deer

READ ABOUT

Early Iroquois people built longhouses that would help shield their communities from the harsh New York winters.

3000 BCE

The first humans make their way to present-day New York

1000 CE

Native Americans arrive in the region

▲ 1300–1400

The Iroquois move into western New York

CHAPTER TWO

FIRST PEOPLE

★

THE EARLIEST RESIDENTS OF WHAT IS NOW NEW YORK WERE HUNTER-GATHERERS WHO LIVED IN CLANS. They made their way to the region about 5,000 years ago. They hunted large game and fished the rivers and lakes. To supplement their food supply, these people collected nuts, wild berries and other fruits, and roots. They moved along with the food supply, setting up temporary villages near the best hunting.

1570 ►
The Iroquois League is formed as the oldest American democracy

LATE 1500s
The Iroquois use longhouses in their communities

▲1714
The Iroquois League admits the Tuscarora as the sixth member

NEW YORK'S NATIVE PEOPLE

When the large game disappeared, the hunter-gatherers changed their lifestyles. They developed methods for hunting small game. Although they still gathered nuts and berries, clans began farming. Remaining in one location during spring, summer, and early fall allowed clans to harvest crops and store food for the winter.

The first Native American people to settle in the region spoke an Algonquian language. They communicated with other groups, which allowed them to trade game, furs, and crafts. Native American tribes arrived in lower New York in about 1000 CE and dominated the area for 300 years. The Mohicans lived along the Hudson River valley. The river provided food and transportation, while the neighboring forests provided game for hunting, fuel for fires, and naturally growing fruits and herbs.

Another Algonquian-language tribe, the Wappinger, settled on Long Island. The Wappinger added mussels, clams, and oysters to their diet. Shellfish was plentiful and easily harvested from the shallows during low tide.

THE LEAGUE OF THE IROQUOIS

Between 1300 and 1400 CE, a group of Iroquois-speaking people moved into western New York. The name *Iroquois* comes from the Algonquian word *Irinakhoiw*, which means "real adders." (Adders are snakes, so this name may have been an insult.) The Iroquois economy was based on farming. Tribes cultivated land, relying on maize (corn), beans, and squash. These crops were called the Three Sisters. Iroquois family units and clans were named after animals, such as wolf, bear, or turtle.

The Iroquois found the game-rich region of central New York ideal for their needs. The first group to settle there evolved into the Seneca tribe. Others soon followed,

FAQ

Q: WHAT IS WAMPUM?

A: Wampum came from the Iroquois and was made of white and purple clamshells. The shells' pattern told the life story of a lost loved one. Only after Europeans began trading with native people did wampum come to represent money.

Native American Peoples

(Before European Contact)

This map shows the general area of Native American peoples before European settlers arrived.

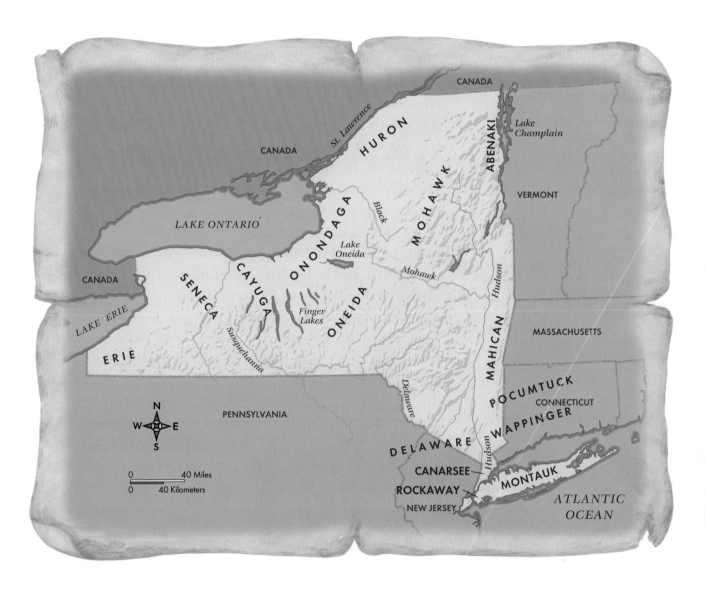

including the Huron, Erie, Cayuga, Onondaga, Oneida, and Mohawk. The tribes traded with each other and occasionally fought each other over hunting territories.

In the middle of the 16th century, a Huron prophet and **shaman** named Deganawidah, the Great Peacemaker, told of a plan that he had seen in a dream for peace among the nations. Among his followers was a young Onondaga warrior named Ayenwatha, who took the prophet's message to each regional tribe. Ayenwatha convinced the Seneca, Onondaga, Oneida, Cayuga, and Mohawk to form a **confederation**. Their agreement formed the League of Five Nations, also known as the Iroquois League.

The Iroquois League said that a league should be able to admit new states as equal members. In 1714 the league admitted the Tuscarora as the sixth member.

The Iroquois League functioned as a confederation of Indian nations. Each of the six nations elected delegates called **sachems**. Sachems governed the grand council of the league. There were 50 sachems, and these men made decisions to lead the nations. If a sachem or leader violated the public trust or opposed the will of the people, women could remove him from office. Then women would select a new representative.

The Iroquois League also required that soldiers select their military officers. If men were to face death on the battlefield, they should choose commanders they trusted.

The league blended the separate nations into a single government to

WORDS TO KNOW

shaman *a Native American spiritual leader*

confederation *an association of groups that come together with common goals*

sachems *representatives of Native American clans*

The Iroquois League is the oldest active democracy in the world.

THE TRIBES OF THE IROQUOIS LEAGUE

TRIBE NAME	IROQUOIAN TERM	MEANING
Seneca	Onondowahgah	People of the Great Hill
Cayuga	Gayogohono	People of the Great Swamp
Onondaga	Onondagega	People of the Hills
Oneida	Onyotaaka	People of the Upright Stone
Mohawk	Kahniakehake	People of the Flint
Tuscarora	Skaruren	Shirt-wearing People

Leaders from the Five Nations (Cayuga, Mohawk, Oneida, Onondaga, and Seneca) assembled around the Huron prophet Deganawidah (center) to recite the laws of the new Iroquois League.

deal with important matters such as peace. Today we call this the federal system, and it is embodied in the United States Constitution. In addition to federalism and elected representatives, the Iroquois League developed other ideas about democratic government that we take for granted today. One was the Algonquin idea of the "powwow"—a meeting to calmly and reasonably discuss issues. Another Algonquin invention was the "caucus," a meeting in which people informally talk through difficult issues. The discussion is kept unemotional and noncombative. The goal of a caucus is to reach an agreement that all parties can accept.

COMMUNITY LIFE

The main social unit of the Iroquois was the mother's family line. The oldest woman in the family was considered the matriarch, a respected elder who settled family disagreements. All real property, such as huts,

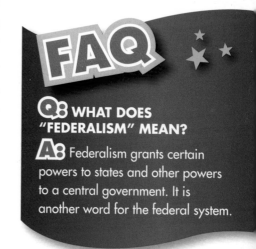

FAQ

Q8 WHAT DOES "FEDERALISM" MEAN?

A8 Federalism grants certain powers to states and other powers to a central government. It is another word for the federal system.

BURYING THE HATCHET

Have you ever wondered where the saying "bury the hatchet" comes from? When the Iroquois League agreed to form a peaceful union, the sachems buried their war axes and other weapons under a white pine as a symbol of peace. According to legend, an underground river washed the weapons away, showing that the peace among the tribes would be long lasting.

WORD TO KNOW

longhouse *a long building used by an entire Native American community*

MINI-BIO

JOANNE SHENANDOAH: SHE SINGS

Joanne Shenandoah (c. 1958—) is a member of the Wolf Clan of the Oneida Nation. Daughter of an Onondaga chief and musician, Shenandoah was given the name Tek-ya-wha-wha, which means "she sings" in the Oneida language. Her style is a blend of pop, folk, classical, and native music, and she has performed at Carnegie Hall, the Kennedy Center, and the White House. A resident of Syracuse, she performed on the 2006 Sacred Ground, which won a Grammy Award for Best Native American Music Album.

 Want to know more? Visit www.factsfornow .scholastic.com and enter the keywords **New York**.

land, or personal goods, belonged to the women. The Haudenosaunee, another name for the Iroquois League, lived in villages of 10 to 50 families, or about 50 to 250 people. By the late 1500s, each village had a **longhouse** for council meetings and ceremonies. A circle of family huts surrounded the longhouse.

Chores were divided between the genders. Men hunted, fished, and protected the village. Women raised children, cooked, sewed, and tended the crops. Women and children planted and harvested corn, beans, squash, and pumpkins.

NATIVE RELIGION

Both Iroquois and Algonquin people believed in the Great Spirit as an all-powerful being. When a corn crop failed or winter was particularly harsh, it was because the Great Spirit was displeased about something. Likewise, if a crop or hunt proved particularly successful, the Great Spirit was showing favor to that tribe.

Long before the Pilgrims held what is generally called the first Thanksgiving, the native people of present-day New York held many such celebrations. Early in the spring, the sugar maple festival thanked the Great Spirit for the gift of maple sap. In early summer, tribes held a strawberry festival, grateful for that fruit. Early fall was the time for the Green Corn Festival, another feast of thanksgiving.

By the time Europeans arrived in the area, native people lived and thrived from the tip of Long Island to Niagara Falls. Their lives followed the patterns of the seasons and nature. No native group could have anticipated the changes that would come with the arrival of the European settlers.

Picture Yourself...

in the Sugar Maple Festival

Spring has finally arrived, and sap is running through the sugar maples. It is almost time for the sugar maple festival. If you are a girl, you work with the other girls and women of the village. You cut into the bark so the sap drips into bowls. Making maple sugar requires gallons of sap. This year, you will take a turn heating rocks and dropping them in the sap to make it boil. This process must be repeated over and over until the sap turns to syrup. As tiring as this might be, the rewards are great. Your tribe depends heavily on maple sugar as a staple food.

Gathering sap from sugar maple trees

READ ABOUT

Henry Hudson arrives along the shore of what becomes known as the Hudson River, in 1609.

1524
▲ Giovanni da Verrazano sails along America's northeast coast

1609
Henry Hudson's Half Moon *sails into New York Bay*

1624
The Dutch West India Company settles New Netherlands colony

CHAPTER THREE

EXPLORATION AND SETTLEMENT

★

IN 1609, ENGLISHMAN HENRY HUDSON, WORKING FOR THE DUTCH, SAILED ACROSS THE ATLANTIC OCEAN, LOOKING FOR A ROUTE TO ASIA. Aboard the ship *Half Moon*, Hudson and his international crew arrived off the coast of Newfoundland. Heading south, Hudson found a wide bay (New York Bay) and began sailing up the river to see if this was, indeed, the hoped-for route. He traveled 150 miles (241 km) north to what is now Albany.

1664

The Duke of York captures New Amsterdam and New Netherlands

▲**1788**

New York becomes the 11th state

1789 ▲

George Washington is sworn in as president in New York City

DUTCH ENCOUNTERS

When the river narrowed, Hudson turned back. Although he did not find the route to Asia, he claimed the land he saw for the Netherlands.

As early as 1614, maps bore the name *Manhattes* for the island of Manhattan. This name came from the word *Manna-hata,* which means "island of many hills" in the Lenape language. The first non-Indian settler of Manhattan was Jan Rodrigues, an African-Portuguese sailor from a Dutch ship.

In 1621, the Dutch government gave the Dutch West India Company permission to organize a permanent settlement on Manhattan Island. The company looked at New Amsterdam as a big moneymaker. It planned to buy furs from native people cheaply and sell them in Europe for huge profits. In 1624, the first Dutch settlers arrived. Some settled on Nut Island (now Governor's Island at the mouth of the Hudson). Others traveled north along the Hudson River to Fort Orange (now Albany).

The Dutch appointed Peter Minuit to serve as governor of the region. Arriving in 1626, Minuit purchased Manhattan Island for $24 in trinkets from the Canarsee Indians and founded the city of New Amsterdam (named for the Dutch city) on it. The Canarsee were pleased with his gifts but did not believe they were selling anything.

MINI-BIO

GIOVANNI DA VERRAZANO: EXPLORER

Like many 16th-century European explorers, Giovanni da Verrazano (c. 1485–c. 1528) crossed the Atlantic Ocean in search of a route to Asia. He sailed along New York's shores in 1524 and wrote of the Native Americans he encountered, "They came toward us very cheerfully, making great shouts of admiration, showing us where we might come to land most safely with our boat." Native Americans pleaded with Verrazano to share his steel weapons, so that they could defend their families, he wrote, "against kidnappers, who frequent the coast to seize and transport them [for sale] to the Spanish islands of the West Indies."

? **Want to know more?** Visit www.factsfornow .scholastic.com and enter the keywords **New York**.

European Exploration of New York

The colored arrows on this map show the routes taken by explorers between 1524 and 1615.

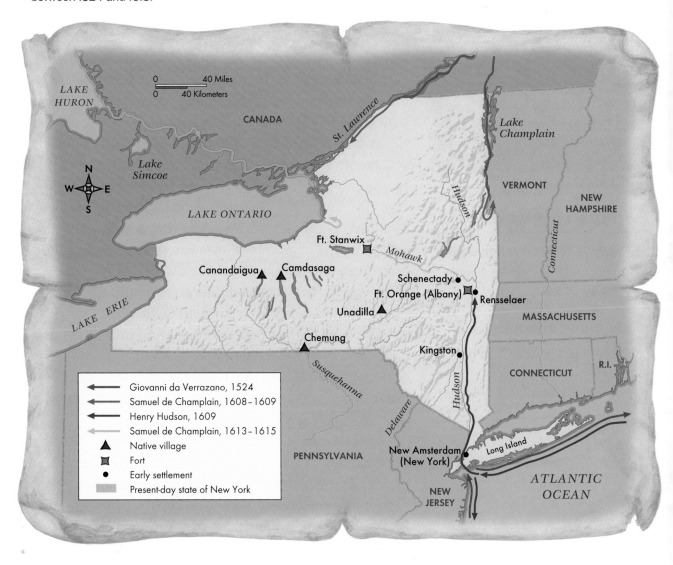

CREWS OF MANY CULTURES

You might think that because Giovanni Verrazano was Italian he had an Italian crew or that the Englishman Henry Hudson had an English crew. In fact, crews represented a mix of languages and cultures. The earliest European captains traveled with Africans, who had special language skills as interpreters with Native Americans.

WORDS TO KNOW

colony *a community settled in a new land but with ties to another government*

indentured servants *people who sign agreements to work for a given amount of time; they are not paid, but receive room and board*

THE DUTCH PATROON SYSTEM

The colony's governors in New Amsterdam were poor administrators seeking to make a fortune. They viewed their Algonquin hosts as enemies not friends, and they favored war over negotiation. Few people wanted to leave the Netherlands to live and work the land in such an uncertain place. The Dutch West India Company awarded five Dutch men parcels of land made up of thousands of acres, because they promised to import new settlers. These five men were called patroons.

Patroons could not settle on Manhattan Island because it was reserved for the West India Company. Instead, they received land grants for property along the Hudson River. The patroons were obliged to establish a **colony** of 50 adults. They could trade in any goods except furs. They were allowed to grow flax or cotton or raise sheep, but they could not weave linen, wool, or cotton cloth. They could sell the raw materials to a mill in the Netherlands to be spun into cloth.

Many of the old patroonships grew into towns and cities that exist today. Jonas Bronck's farm became the Bronx. Adriaen Van der Donck founded Yonkers in 1646. The city took its name from Van der Donck's title, *jonkeer*, which means "young gentleman."

New Amsterdam's worst problem was attracting laborers. The Dutch West India Company resorted to forced labor. The company imported European men and women as **indentured servants**. Laborers from Ireland, Denmark, Sweden, Germany, Norway, and France soon began to come ashore in New Amsterdam. They served a term of about seven years, and then left to make money in the fur trade or on their own farms.

In 1626, the Dutch brought 11 enslaved African men to New Amsterdam, followed two years later with the arrival of three enslaved African women. Africans constructed Fort Amsterdam, cleared land, cut wood for homes, and built roads. They built a defensive wall on the southern end of Manhattan Island and widened an Algonquin path into a major road. Some African men and women became servants in the homes of the wealthy, and others harvested the crops that fed the people of New Amsterdam.

While slaves in British and Spanish colonies faced harsh and cruel conditions, Dutch New Amsterdam developed a milder form of slavery. Africans could earn the same wages as whites and looked forward to gaining freedom for their children. Africans were welcomed into a Dutch church that blessed their marriages, baptized their children, and offered them Christian burials. They were able to own and inherit property and even sue in Dutch courts.

In 1646, Peter Stuyvesant arrived as the new governor of what was now New Netherlands, extending up the Hudson River and including parts of New Jersey and Long Island. Stuyvesant ruled his colony with an iron hand. He banned cursing or selling weapons and liquor to the Algonquin. He imposed heavy taxes on imported goods, and insisted everyone strictly observe Sunday as a holy day. In 1652, the colony's first Jewish citizens were not welcomed by Stuyvesant. He called them "hateful enemies" and tried to bar them. The Dutch West India Company in the Netherlands overruled him, but it took two years for Jews to be admitted.

By 1660, the Netherlands had turned New Amsterdam into a major shipping center. Cloth, printed matter, and furniture arrived in the port to be traded for beaver, mink, lumber, and other raw materials. But the biggest business was the slave trade.

Manhattan's Wall Street, today's center of international finance, is named for the wooden fence that Africans built in 1653 as New Amsterdam's northern boundary.

LAND OF MANY LANGUAGES

In 1643, Peter Stuyvesant's predecessor Governor Wilhelm Kieft heard "men of 18 different languages" in New Amsterdam. He specifically mentioned Walloons (French-speaking Belgians), Italians, Irish, English, a Moroccan Muslim called "Turk," French Huguenots, Danes, Lithuanians, and a Czech. (There were also Dutch and African people, though he didn't mention them.) There were many religions represented, as well. There were Catholics, Puritans, Lutherans, Anabaptists, and Mennonites.

THE BRITISH PRESENCE

Great Britain, having established profitable colonies to the north and south, resented the successful trade of the Netherlands, a smaller nation, and wanted to control the New Netherland colony. The problem was that the Dutch traded not only with Europe, but also with the British colonies. In 1663, Dutch trade had eaten away at British profits, and taking New Netherland became essential to the British. James, the Duke of York and King Charles II's brother, sent four warships to New Amsterdam in 1664. Stuyvesant surrendered New Amsterdam to Britain's Colonel Richard Nicolls, who became the colony's first British governor.

So a New Netherlands that extended up the Hudson and beyond Albany became New York. Only about 30 percent of its 7,000 people were Dutch. The rest were a mosaic of colors, nationalities, and religions, including 700 slaves and about 70 free Africans.

The slave market on Pearl Street in New York City, 1700s

The British rulers were determined to make their colony an international success. The Duke of York held a controlling interest in the Royal African Company and envisioned New York as a huge slave market. The slave market at Wall Street was the biggest in the city. More than 100 of the city's 400 merchants dealt in slaves. Their business interests were increasingly tied to cotton and sugar plantations in the south and the Caribbean, which relied on slave labor.

In New York, the number of slaves increased faster than the white population. In some counties, one-third of the people were slaves. The colony had more slaves than any other in British North America. The Dutch milder form of slavery was replaced by a harsh, profit-driven bondage. The value of slaves rose and their conditions worsened. New laws sought to prevent escapes and rebellions. Clergymen wanted to educate slave men and women, but owners feared education would stir revolt.

Enslaved men and women worked alongside white servants in fields, in homes, or at the docks. Some were skilled carpenters, cooks, weavers, and printers. As New York prospered, some people became wealthy, while others sank into poverty. White workers and farmers along the Hudson River became discontented. Conflict was common as farmers in the Hudson valley rebelled against high rents and unfair landlords. In New York City, tailors and other workers went on **strike** against low wages. Middle-class citizens also began to challenge British colonial rule.

WORD TO KNOW

strike *an organized refusal to work, usually as a sign of protest about working conditions*

WAR FOR INDEPENDENCE

By the 1760s, colonists had begun to unite against British rule and taxes. In 1765, the British passed the

Stamp Act, taxing all colonial printed materials, from books and deeds to accounts of grocery bills and even playing cards. Colonists were outraged. That year, delegates from nine colonies met in the Stamp Act Congress in New York City. They called themselves "The First Congress of the American Colonies in Opposition to the Tyrannical Acts of the British Parliament." Their demand for "inherent rights and liberties" pushed the 13 colonies toward independence.

In 1776, the colonists declared themselves a separate nation, independent of Great Britain. New Yorkers Lewis Morris, Francis Lewis, Philip Livingston, and William Floyd signed the Declaration of Independence. To achieve this independence, the infant states fought Great Britain in the American Revolutionary War (1775–1783). The British recognized that New York played a strategic role in the colonies. If the British could take New York, communications and troop movements among the newly formed rebellious states would be difficult.

New York State became the principal battleground of the Revolution—a third of the battles were fought there. One of the most important victories came when General Horatio Gates commanded the American troops in the Battle of Saratoga. The Americans successfully outsmarted Britain's General John Burgoyne in September 1777 and again in October. Ten days later, Burgoyne surrendered to Gates. This battle proved to be a turning point in the war. France began to think that America had a chance to win. Shortly after Saratoga, the French sent money, supplies, troops, and ships to help the American side. The British finally admitted defeat with the surrender of General Charles Cornwallis to General George Washington on October 14, 1781, in Yorktown, Virginia.

SEE IT HERE!

FRAUNCES TAVERN

Fraunces Tavern in New York City was built in 1719 and converted to a tavern in 1763. The Sons of Liberty, a secret society of rebels, met there before the American Revolution. Although the war ended in 1781, British troops occupied New York City until 1783. George Washington celebrated with his officers at Fraunces Tavern after forcing the British to leave New York. Today, see the room where the Sons of Liberty planned their rebellion and where Washington bade farewell to his officers in 1783.

New York: From Territory to Statehood

(1609–1788)

This map shows the original New York colony and the area (in yellow) that became the state of New York in 1788.

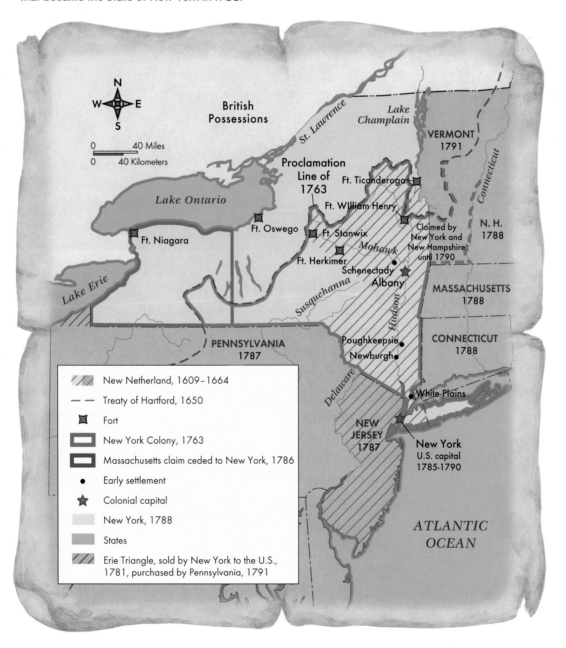

- New Netherland, 1609–1664
- Treaty of Hartford, 1650
- Fort
- New York Colony, 1763
- Massachusetts claim ceded to New York, 1786
- Early settlement
- Colonial capital
- New York, 1788
- States
- Erie Triangle, sold by New York to the U.S., 1781, purchased by Pennsylvania, 1791

George Washington (second from left) speaks with an Iroquois chief. The Founding Fathers incorporated some aspects of the Iroquois political system into the U.S. government.

A NEW NATION

In June 1776, before signing the Declaration of Independence, the Continental Congress had welcomed a delegation of Iroquois chiefs. Benjamin Franklin had been the first of the Founding Fathers to study the Iroquois League. He was so impressed that he advocated use of its political structure of federalism. Thomas Paine, George Washington, Thomas Jefferson, and other Founding Fathers became fascinated with Indian political institutions. They visited Native American villages and studied their political theories.

In 1781, the states accepted the Articles of Confederation, a loose agreement that recognized specific states' rights, formed a mutual defense, and set up a federal government. But the Articles of Confederation did not work. By 1787, the Constitutional Convention was ready to adopt more of the Iroquois League's ideas. The Founding Fathers discovered that the Iroquois followed better procedures than the British Parliament, whose delegates interrupted one another or shouted out disagreements. Among the Iroquois, one person spoke at a time and there were no noisy interruptions or shouting. The purpose of a debate was to persuade and educate, not to confront or put down an opponent. Another feature of the Constitution came from the Algonquin right of **impeachment**, which the Indians had granted to women. Women's rights and impeachment were both new ideas to Europeans. Delegates voted to place impeachment in the Constitution but not power for women.

The new U.S. Constitution also invited new states to enter the Union as equals, following the example the league had set by inviting the Tuscarora to join. Under federal principles, each new state would be given an equal voice with the original 13 states.

Taking the Iroquois League as a model, the U.S. Constitution was completed in 1787. The following year, New York ratified the Constitution and became the 11th state of the new nation. New York City became the temporary capital of the United States. At a meeting of Congress, George Washington was elected president. Favoring the Iroquois League over European tradition, the Constitution declared that civilians, not military officers, should control the armed forces. So the general who had led the colonies to freedom was not a general anymore. Washington took his oath of office in April 1789 in New York City, on the balcony of Federal Hall on Wall Street. New York's Robert R. Livingston administered the oath of office to the president. A new nation had been created, and both the Iroquois League and New York State had played a huge role in its making.

WORD TO KNOW

impeachment *the act of charging a political official with misconduct while in office, sometimes resulting in removal from office*

READ ABOUT

The New York Central and Hudson River Railroad was instrumental in establishing New York as the country's financial leader.

▲1792

The New York Stock Exchange is created

▲1825

The Erie Canal unites all of New York with the Great Lakes states

1827

Slavery is abolished in New York

CHAPTER FOUR

GROWTH AND CHANGE

★

WHEN GEORGE WASHINGTON CALLED NEW YORK "THE SEAT OF THE EMPIRE" IN 1784, HE MUST HAVE HAD A VISION OF THE STATE'S FUTURE ECONOMIC GROWTH. With advances in transportation, its countryside became "the breadbasket of the nation." New York City became the financial center of the new country.

1848

Women gather in Seneca Falls for the first women's rights convention

1886 ▸

The Statue of Liberty is unveiled in New York Harbor

1902 ▸

New York City's Flatiron Building, the first skyscraper, opens for business

The New York Stock Exchange was housed in this building at 40 Wall Street until it moved into its current building in 1903.

TRANSPORTATION AND TRADE

In 1792, the New York Stock Exchange was established in New York City. It allowed people to invest money in various businesses. The Stock Exchange attracted banks and businesses to the city, which generated continued growth.

As citizens moved into the western parts of the state, the number of products—flour, wheat, corn, and fruit—marketed through New York City grew. Getting those products to market required improved transportation. Laborers and engineers built a network of turnpikes to connect New York to major cities throughout the region. However, roads were not paved, and heavy rain would turn a road into mud. River travel was cheaper and more reliable.

In the early 1800s, it became obvious that New York needed cheaper, safer transportation to bring goods from the western regions to New York City. The solution was to connect Lake Erie to the Hudson River by means of a canal. Construction took eight years. During that time, builders developed 18 **aqueducts** to carry the canal over ravines and rivers, as well as 83 **locks** to raise the water 568 feet (173 m) between the Hudson River and Lake Erie. The canal was a mere 4 feet (1.2 m) deep—deep enough to tow barges along the river with the aid of horses, mules, or oxen. During its most productive years, the Erie Canal was enlarged three times to make way for the tons of cargo it carried.

Rail travel, introduced in the United States in the early 1800s, expanded to connect many New York cities. The Mohawk and Hudson Railroad, running between Albany and Schenectady, received its charter in 1826. After five years of laying track, the railroad opened. It would later become part of the New York Central Railroad line. During the 1830s, railroads connected Ithaca and Owego, New York City and Harlem, and points north, south, and west.

INDUSTRY AND CHANGE

The industries of banking, shipping, railroad transportation, and manufacturing made millionaires out of men such as John D. Rockefeller, John Jacob Astor, and J.

WORDS TO KNOW

aqueducts *structures for carrying large amounts of flowing water*

locks *enclosures in canals with gates on each end that help boats pass from level to level*

WORD TO KNOW

persecution *mistreatment of people because of their beliefs*

A colorized photo of an Italian immigrant woman and her children arriving at Ellis Island in New York City

Pierpont Morgan. But not every New Yorker became rich. But white workers made up half of New York City's population and yet they owned a small percent of its wealth. They worked long hours at low pay and were crowded into slums of small wooden houses. In Manhattan's Five Points slum, Irish immigrants and African Americans endured unemployment, disease, and crime. It was one of many poor neighborhoods in the state.

Business leaders took advantage of the influx of immigrants pouring into the cities from Europe as cheap labor. People came from Ireland, England, Poland, Russia, Italy, and Greece. Men worked in construction, building bridges, canals, and railroads. Women worked as chambermaids, cooks, or child caregivers. Factories employed immigrant labor, demanding long hours and paying low wages. Immigrants came to escape hunger, poverty, and religious **persecution**. These new arrivals brought with them their music, languages, customs, and foods from Europe. Many worked hard to learn English, find jobs, and become American citizens with the right to vote and hold office.

New York's free people of color also increased in numbers and skills. James Durham paid for his freedom, learned to speak several languages, and became a noted physician. Other free people became teachers, ministers, or mechanics. Many bought their own homes or businesses. By the 1820s, a dozen black congregations owned or rented buildings in Manhattan. Soon many African American communities had churches and charitable and educational societies.

REFORM MOVEMENTS

Many religious and reform movements began to sweep Upstate New York in the 1820s and 1830s, particularly between Troy and Buffalo. Sunday Schools, orphanages, and temperance groups (opposing liquor) were started. Reformers created "**Utopian** communities" in Oneida and Skaneateles, where families cooperated with others to share work and food. While the Utopian communities eventually came to an end, two reform movements would change the course of not only New York but also U.S. history. These were the campaigns against slavery and for women's rights.

Abolition

Many New Yorkers wanted to end the slave trade and human bondage. In 1800, these **abolitionists** persuaded the New York legislature to pass an **emancipation** law that would go into effect in 1827. Meanwhile, most slaves continued to do New York's hard work. A third of New York City's households either owned slaves or hired free black laborers, and Brooklyn had a larger percentage of slaves than South Carolina. Other enslaved New Yorkers would not wait until 1827. They fled bondage by heading north to Canada. An Underground Railroad of safehouses, called stations, and people who acted as "conductors" aided their flight. In Troy, Syracuse, Rochester, and other upstate towns, people of both races risked their lives to help.

PUBLIC EDUCATION

New York public education started in 1787 with the opening of the African Free Schools for former slaves. The schools were a project of the state's Manumission Society, founded after the Revolution by government leaders who wanted to end slavery. Hundreds of boys and girls learned reading, writing, job skills, and Christian beliefs from white teachers in African Free Schools. Graduates often became prominent New York activists, teachers, and intellectuals.

WORDS TO KNOW

Utopian *describing a society that is ideal and perfect*

abolitionists *people who were opposed to slavery and worked to end it*

emancipation *the act of freeing slaves from bondage*

MINI-BIO

DAVID RUGGLES: FREEDOM FIGHTER

In 1827, the year of New York's emancipation, David Ruggles (1810–1849) arrived in the city and opened a successful grocery store. Together with black educators James McCune Smith and Charles B. Ray, and writer Philip Bell, he formed a Vigilance Committee to fight slave catchers. Their committee helped 300 people escape in their first year and 366 the next year. Ruggles alone aided 300 men, women, and children to safety, including statesman-to-be Frederick Douglass.

Ruggles opened the city's first black bookstore and turned his home into an African American history library. One time he was jailed and another time his bookstore was burned down. But Ruggles never slowed down. His home became an Underground Railroad station and he helped guide runaways to freedom. He was jailed several more times, but he continued to battle for liberty.

? Want to know more? Visit www.factsfornow.scholastic.com and enter the keywords **New York**.

In 1821, a new state constitution extended the vote to all white men, and it allowed black men to vote only if they owned $250 in property. Few people owned that much. State Black Laws denied people of color the right to run for office, testify against a white person, or serve on a jury. To end these injustices, African Americans met in protest conventions. But the march to equality was very slow.

In 1827, emancipation finally came to New York. The 30,000 people of color in the state now could go as they wished and live where they chose. To help **fugitives**, free people of color across the state

WORD TO KNOW

fugitives *people who are trying to flee or escape*

Here is a proposal for Frederick Douglass's *North Star*. This antislavery newspaper would serve as a strong force for the abolitionist movement.

PROSPECTUS

FOR AN ANTI-SLAVERY PAPER, TO BE ENTITLED

NORTH STAR.

FREDERICK DOUGLASS

Proposes to publish, in ROCHESTER, N. Y., a **WEEKLY ANTI-SLAVERY PAPER**, with the above title.

The object of the NORTH STAR will be to attack SLAVERY in all its forms and aspects; advocate UNIVERSAL EMANCIPATION; exalt the standard of PUBLIC MORALITY; promote the Moral and Intellectual Improvement of the COLORED PEOPLE; and hasten the day of FREEDOM to the Three Millions of our ENSLAVED FELLOW COUNTRYMEN.

The Paper will be printed upon a double medium sheet, at $2,00 per annum, if paid in advance, or $2,50, if payment be delayed over six months.

The names of Subscribers may be sent to the following named persons, and should be forwarded, as far as practicable, by the first of November, proximo.

FREDERICK DOUGLASS, Lynn, Mass.
SAMUEL BROOKE, Salem, Ohio.
M. R. DELANY, Pittsburgh, Pa.
VALENTINE NICHOLSON, Harveysburgh, Warren Co. O.
Mr. WALCOTT, 21 Cornhill, Boston.

JOEL P. DAVIS, Economy, Wayne County, Ind.
CHRISTIAN DONALDSON, Cincinnati, Ohio.
J. M. M'KIM, Philadelphia, Pa.
AMARANCY PAINE, Providence, R. I.
Mr. GAY, 142 Nassau Street, New York.

SUBSCRIBERS' NAMES.	RESIDENCE.	NO. OF COPIES.

mobilized—William W. Brown in Buffalo, Reverend Thomas James in Rochester, Reverend Jermain Loguen in Syracuse, Harriet Tubman in Auburn, Sojourner Truth in Hurley and Kingston. New York's antislavery movement grew stronger after 1838 when Frederick Douglass fled bondage in Maryland and reached New York City. Douglass became a leading antislavery writer and orator, an advocate of women's rights, an Underground Railroad conductor, and in time a presidential adviser.

Women's Rights

When Frederick Douglass moved his family to Rochester to publish his *North Star* newspaper, he knew he would be among friends. Since 1835, Rochester had a female antislavery society organized by Susan B. Anthony, Elizabeth Cady Stanton, Amy Post, and Sojourner Truth. In addition to fighting against human bondage, these women organized societies to promote equality of the sexes. At the time, women were not allowed to vote. Once married, a woman's property became the property of her husband. Education for women was limited; few women became doctors, and fewer still became lawyers, judges, or religious ministers. What women wanted was simple: rights equal to those enjoyed by men.

MINI-BIO

SOJOURNER TRUTH: VOICE OF FREEDOM

Isabella Baumfree (1797–1883) was a slave born in Hurley. She was kept from learning to read and write, often beaten, and sold four times. When her son Peter was taken from her and sold, she fled with her baby to a white neighbor who agreed to purchase her. Then she won the return of Peter in a lawsuit. After she escaped to freedom in 1826, she changed her name to Sojourner Truth. In 1850, *The Narrative of Sojourner Truth: A Northern Slave* was published. She toured the country speaking out against slavery and held audiences spellbound as she told of her struggle for liberty. Truth also joined the women's rights movement and became one of its leaders.

? Want to know more? Visit www.factsfornow .scholastic.com and enter the keywords **New York**.

WOW

In 1851, Elizabeth Smith Miller shocked the people of Seneca Falls by appearing in public in pants. The pants were soon called "bloomers" after Amelia Jenks Bloomer, who popularized the style in her Seneca Falls newspaper.

This statue of women's rights leaders is displayed at the Women's Rights National Historical Park Visitor Center in Seneca Falls.

MINI-BIO

SUSAN B. ANTHONY: A VOICE FOR WOMEN

Susan B. Anthony (1820–1906) had a strong sense of justice. She believed that women should be treated equal to men under the law. Early in her life, she fought against slavery. Anthony joined the women's rights movement in 1852. She campaigned across the country for women's right to vote. She persuaded the University of Rochester to admit women—a scandalous idea at the time. The trustees agreed but worried about the cost. Anthony raised $50,000 and forced the school's trustees to live up to their promise. Anthony died 14 years before the 19th Amendment to the U.S. Constitution was passed, giving women throughout the United States the right to vote.

Want to know more? Visit www.factsfornow .scholastic.com and enter the keywords **New York**.

In 1848, these women gathered in Seneca Falls, New York, for the first women's rights convention in the United States. When delegates wrote a women's Declaration of Independence, Stanton insisted it demand a woman's right to vote. She asked her husband to second her motion, and he refused. Then she turned to Frederick Douglass, who seconded her motion. It passed.

The National Woman Suffrage Association wanted an amendment to the U.S. Constitution giving women the right to vote. In 1872, Susan B. Anthony voted in the presidential election in Rochester, New York—and was promptly arrested. The battle for women's rights would continue into the 20th century, and New York would be at the center of the movement.

CIVIL WAR

In 1808, Congress had outlawed the importation of slaves, but there was so much money in it that the trade continued illegally. New York bankers and merchants and southern slaveholders depended on one another, and New York politicians rarely opposed slavery itself. New Yorkers who traded with southern slaveholders encouraged newspaper attacks on abolitionist speakers and sometimes made it dangerous to attend antislavery meetings.

In 1850, Congress passed the Fugitive Slave Law of 1850, requiring federal officers to return any runaway slave found in a northern state. It also required citizens to help the officers who sought escaped slaves. Black and white abolitionists formed groups to protect African Americans from Buffalo to Brooklyn. This infuriated southern slaveholders.

The slavery debate came to a head in the presidential election of 1860. Two major issues in that year's election were states' rights and abolition. In February, a candidate named Abraham Lincoln came to New York City to give a speech against slavery, and his campaign took off. Many voters believed that Lincoln would bring about an end to slavery, prompting Southern states to withdraw from the Union after he won the election. About a month after his inauguration, the North and South were at war. The Civil War (1861–1865) had started.

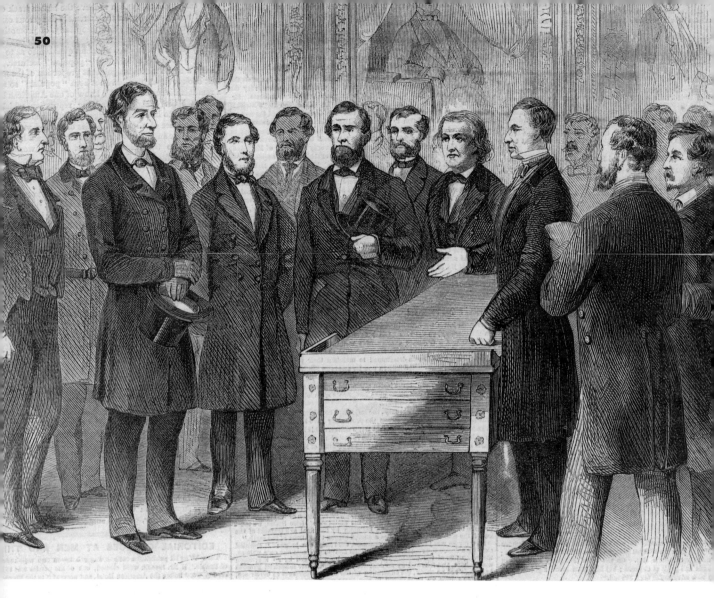

Fernando Wood (standing at desk), the mayor of New York City, greets President Abraham Lincoln (holding hat with hands crossed) at City Hall. Lincoln visited New York City in 1861 to speak out against the expansion of slavery.

The Civil War found New York deeply divided. In New York City, Mayor Fernando Wood represented businessmen with a vital economic interest in the Southern Confederacy. He proposed the city remain neutral so it could trade with both sides, or perhaps secede from the Union. On the other hand, 465,000 New Yorkers took up arms for the Union army. In addition to soldiers, New York supplied many of the goods needed to win the war. Many New York women worked for the war effort in factories or served as nurses in the field.

In 1863, a new Draft Law triggered New York City's worst riot. The draft required men to join the military. But rich men were allowed to hire substitutes to fight for them for $300. This policy infuriated the city's poor, including many Irish and other recent immigrants. The war, they shouted, was "a rich man's war and a poor man's fight." Roving white mobs surged through streets and avenues killing, destroying, and robbing. The rioters did not disperse until the arrival of four Union regiments from the front. More than 100 people died that week in the largest urban upheaval in U.S. history.

A shrewd, corrupt politician named William M. "Boss" Tweed realized that he could gain a lot of political power from the city's frustrated immigrant groups. By the end of the Civil War in 1865, Boss Tweed's Tammany Hall, an arm of the Democratic Party, dominated New York City politics. The Tammany machine spent funds recklessly and selfishly. And Tweed, who had promised to improve conditions for the immigrant poor, became a rich man. Newspaper cartoonist Thomas Nast, a German immigrant who depicted Tweed as a bloated crook, finally brought down Tweed's corrupt rule. Tweed was convicted of fraud, was sent to jail, and died there.

A NEW CENTURY

During the war, women had run homes and businesses, succeeded at what had traditionally been considered "men's work," and experienced a new sense of freedom. When men returned from the war, many women were not willing to give up their new roles. They wanted their rights and intended to carry on the mission begun in Seneca Falls in 1848.

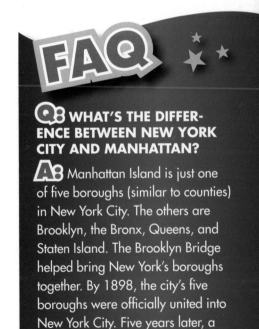

Q8 WHAT'S THE DIFFERENCE BETWEEN NEW YORK CITY AND MANHATTAN?

A8 Manhattan Island is just one of five boroughs (similar to counties) in New York City. The others are Brooklyn, the Bronx, Queens, and Staten Island. The Brooklyn Bridge helped bring New York's boroughs together. By 1898, the city's five boroughs were officially united into New York City. Five years later, a subway system helped cement their connections.

THE STATUE OF LIBERTY

During the American Revolution, the nations of France and the United States formed a great friendship. So 100 years later, in 1876, French sculptor Frederic-Auguste Bartholdi took on the task of creating a gift to mark U.S. independence. The result was the Statue of Liberty, which was completed in 1884. The following year, it was shipped to the United States in 350 pieces, packed in 214 crates. Then, over the course of four months, in was reassembled on a pedestal (supplied by the United States) overlooking New York Harbor. And on October 28, 1886, the statue was dedicated in front of a crowd of thousands. "The New Colossus," a poem by Emma Lazarus, is on the statue's pedestal. Part of it reads: "Give me your tired, your poor, your huddled masses yearning to breathe free." Over the next decades, the statue served as a beacon of hope for people who came to the United States to start new lives.

As the 20th century approached, great changes made transportation and communication easier. The number of railroad lines in the nation doubled after the Civil War. Travel from New York to San Francisco took days rather than weeks or months. Telephones, invented in 1876, allowed quick, easy communication for businesses and individuals. In 1885, phone

The Statue of Liberty was a gift from France to celebrate 100 years of U.S. independence.

A great fireworks demonstration took place on the evening of May 24, 1883, celebrating the opening of the Brooklyn Bridge. On completion, it was the largest suspension bridge in the world.

A FAMILY AFFAIR

For many years, millions of people have crossed the Brooklyn Bridge without ever thinking about the tremendous family effort that went into building it. John Roebling was born in Prussia (now Germany) and came to America in 1831. In the mid-1800s, people crossed from Brooklyn to Manhattan by ferry. A trained engineer, Roebling designed the Brooklyn Bridge and convinced investors to back the project.

While he was surveying the site, his foot was crushed, and he developed tetanus, which led to his death. His son, Washington Roebling, took over building the bridge. However, when he went underwater in a caisson, a container that allowed the men to work underwater, he developed the bends (nitrogen narcosis). The bends left him paralyzed, unable to speak, and partially blind. His wife, Emily Roebling, took over on-site supervision of the construction. The Brooklyn Bridge opened in 1883, and it was, at that time, the longest suspension bridge in the world.

lines connected New York and Philadelphia. Seven years later, calls could be made between New York and Chicago. The cost for the first five minutes was $9—a fortune at the time. At the turn of the century, many people had phones not only where they worked, but also in their homes. In 1883, the magnificent Brooklyn Bridge was completed. And in 1886, France presented the United States with a wonderful gift: the Statue of Liberty. This symbol of freedom still graces New York Harbor. In 1902, the Flatiron Building, the first skyscraper, opened in New York City. It was a time of rapid growth, and New York's future looked bright.

54

READ ABOUT

The stitching and fitting department of a shoe factory in Syracuse, in the 1920s

1917
New York women gain the right to vote

1920s
The Harlem Renaissance takes place

◄1931
The Empire State Building is completed

CHAPTER FIVE

MORE MODERN TIMES

★

As the 20th century dawned, millions of Europeans entered the United States through Ellis Island. Their arrival spurred factories and farms throughout New York and the nation. The state enjoyed healthy agricultural harvests, selling produce and canned products worldwide. Factories became highly productive, and New York City produced 10 percent of the nation's manufacturing output.

1952
The United Nations meets for the first time in its new headquarters in Manhattan

2001
A terrorist attack on the United States destroys the World Trade Center

2012
Hurricane Sandy devastates New York City and the surrounding area

People from all over the world sell their wares at the Mulberry Street Market in New York City's Lower East Side in the early 1900s.

IMMIGRANTS TO NEW YORK

Most newcomers came from eastern and southern Europe, and a few came from Asia. Hundreds of thousands of Jews and Italians came across the Atlantic, while most Chinese came by way of California. By 1910, Jews made up more than one-fourth of New York City's population; Italians made up one-sixth. In Manhattan, they settled on the Lower East Side in nearby neighborhoods.

New immigrants formed similar ethnic neighborhoods in cities throughout the state. Their first task in their new communities was to build houses of worship. Then they developed educational centers, started newspapers, and entered politics. Most newcomers wanted their children to learn English and American ways. They enrolled their children in public schools. Parents were also eager to learn English, citizenship, and city trades.

Earlier Protestant immigrants often viewed the new immigrants suspiciously, even though they generated enormous wealth for their employers. Most immigrants worked in factories. For five or six cents an hour, they labored 12 hours a day, with only Sundays off. Women and children were paid even less. Industrial accidents were common. To demand decent pay and protect their rights, immigrants formed unions. On Manhattan's Lower East Side, strikes against shop owners were common and strikers frequently clashed with police.

People tried to live in peace with their neighbors, but conflicts sometimes erupted. In 1900, an argument between a white policeman and a black man in midtown Manhattan led to a police attack on African American men. Many black people decided to move uptown to Harlem where they would be safe. In a few years, a new subway system made this easier. Others moved to Brooklyn, Queens, Long Island, or upstate.

WAR AND STRUGGLE

World War I (1914–1918) brought dramatic social and political changes. Women nationwide gained the right to vote. A vast African American migration from southern states arrived in northern cities. In New York City, dockworkers went on strike in 1918, followed the next year by a trolley car operators' strike in Buffalo, and a machinists' strike in Schenectady. The year 1919 was a violent one, with 24 race riots. **Inflation**, which reduced the buying power of workers' dollars, was rampant after the war.

WORD TO KNOW

inflation *a condition in which the prices of goods increase faster than wages*

EARLY RADIO AND TV

Schenectady is the home of General Electric's WGY-AM, one of the country's first commercial radio stations. There in 1928 General Electric produced the first regular television broadcasts in the United States. Experimental station W2XB began regular broadcasts on Thursday and Friday afternoons. This pioneer station, now called WRGB, is the capital district's CBS affiliate.

WORD TO KNOW

civil rights *basic rights that are guaranteed to all people under the U.S. Constitution*

In the 1920s, Marcus Garvey was a symbol for African American unity and pride.

THE HARLEM RENAISSANCE

In the 1920s, New York City became the first home of the new media—the movie, recording, and radio industries. At the same time, Harlem became a home and cultural center for African Americans. Every major black church, business, and **civil rights** organization opened an office in Harlem. Of the tens of thousands who moved in, 50,000 had come from the West Indies.

In the 1920s, Marcus Garvey, a Jamaican immigrant, made Harlem the headquarters of his "Back to Africa" movement and declared himself the provisional president of Africa. Touring the United States, he preached a message of black pride and empowerment. U.S. government officials who disagreed with Garvey had him arrested, jailed, and deported to Jamaica. Though his movement collapsed, Garvey had shown African Americans how their unity could lead to political power.

Harlem also became a cultural center for people of African descent. Black musicians, playwrights, novelists, poets, dancers, visual artists, blues singers, and actors created a "Harlem Renaissance." Their works celebrated the lost history and creative past of African people. Through books, paintings, records, radio, and theater, the Harlem Renaissance shaped culture throughout New York, the United States, and the world.

A central figure during the Harlem Renaissance was Arturo Schomburg. Born in Puerto Rico, he came to New York City in 1891. He was a writer and social activist who thought it was important to preserve African American history. In 1911, he founded the Negro Society for Historical Research. He went on to gather a vast collection of African materials and documents. In 1926, the New York Public Library made his collection part of its Harlem branch, and Schomburg oversaw it until his death in 1938. Today, the Schomburg Center for Research in Black Culture, part of the New York Public Library, is an acclaimed research library, with more than 10 million items.

THE CRASH AND THE GREAT DEPRESSION

The Great Depression deepened with the Wall Street Stock Market crash in 1929 and forever changed New York. Families lost their jobs and savings, and could not pay their mortgages or rent. By the time the Empire State Building opened in 1931, few companies could afford its high rents.

In 1932, former New York governor Franklin Roosevelt was elected president. Faced with the difficult task of bringing the United States out of the Depression, he told Americans, "The only thing we have to fear is fear itself." His confidence and his New Deal programs began to bring relief to starving families and put people back to work.

In New York, the New Deal provided money to build bridges, libraries, and schools. New York City mayor Fiorello LaGuardia oversaw 1,700 projects, from jungle gyms in parks to the Central Park Zoo, from East River Drive to a hospital in Queens.

When the Empire State Building was completed in 1931, it was the tallest building in the world.

SEE IT HERE!

HISTORIC HYDE PARK

Experience the lives of New York's famous Roosevelt family at Hyde Park, New York. Visit the home of Franklin and Eleanor Roosevelt called Val-Kill (Dutch for "valley stream") to get a taste of how they lived and where they worked. The Henry Wallace Educational Center holds the former president's library and thousands of Roosevelt documents. Val-Kill was a comfortable, family-style retreat where the Roosevelts and their children had picnics and swam. Walk through Stone Cottage, once a furniture factory that Eleanor began, and see the home she converted for herself after her husband died.

MINI-BIO

FIORELLO LAGUARDIA: NEW YORK CITY MAYOR

Italians had been a part of New York life since explorer Verrazano. But prejudice had denied them political power. In 1934, New York City elected East Harlem's congressman Fiorello LaGuardia (1882–1947) its first Italian mayor. A short, pudgy Episcopalian with a Jewish mother, LaGuardia spoke a dozen languages. A strong supporter of the New Deal and unions, he also opened new parks, improved education, and urged young people to read. During a newspaper strike, he read the comics pages over the radio.

 Want to know more? Visit www.factsfornow.scholastic.com and enter the keywords **New York**.

ECONOMIC UPS AND DOWNS

During the Depression, a group of business leaders got together and organized a New York World's Fair. Four years later, in 1939–1940, this event allowed visitors to imagine what the world of the future would be like. Exhibits included a huge globe, one of the first televisions, and a futuristic car. (The site in Queens was used for another World's Fair in 1964–1965.)

When World War II broke out in Europe in 1939, jobs increased across the United States. American factories produced aircraft, engines, naval ships, machine guns, and tanks that were all sold to England and France. In December 1941, following the Japanese attack on Pearl Harbor, the United States was compelled to enter the war. By this time, most New Yorkers had work. As men enlisted in the military, more women took over their jobs in factories and on farms.

The war changed New York. Harlem elected Adam Clayton Powell Jr. its first African American city councilman, and then elected him to Congress. In 1946, New York became the first state to pass a law against racial discrimination in housing. When the new United Nations opened its headquarters on the East River in 1956, it welcomed diplomats from Africa, South America, and Asia. In the first great migration by plane, Puerto Ricans began to arrive in New York.

Ed Sullivan (left) talks with film star Gina Lollobrigida and Rear Admiral Roscoe Hillenkoetter on the set of *Toast of the Town*, one of the many TV shows that filmed in New York during the 1950s.

East Harlem changed from an Italian neighborhood to El Barrio (which means "neighborhood"), a center of Hispanic American life and culture.

In New York, the 1950s and 1960s became a golden era for many. Television replaced radio as the primary source of family entertainment, and New York City studios produced most of the shows on TV. Broadway shows such as *The King and I, My Fair Lady,* and *Death of a Salesman* packed theaters. Publishing houses introduced a cheaper book for the mass market: the paperback novel.

While New York's economy flourished, many of its citizens did not. But social improvements cost money and affected the state's economy. Throughout the 1960s and early 1970s, high taxes caused many companies, including the steel and automotive industries, to leave New York. New York City lost jobs in fashion, printing, banking, and manufacturing.

MALCOLM X: ACTIVIST

Malcolm Little (1925–1965) was born into a family that believed in Marcus Garvey's dream of a better world for people of color. During a stint in jail for petty crimes, Little joined the Nation of Islam and became Malcolm X. Placed in command of New York's leading Muslim mosque, he took his campaign for justice and equality onto the streets of Harlem. At first, he criticized the civil rights movement for seeking integration. But after he met the nonviolent Martin Luther King Jr. and others in the southern struggle, he changed his mind.

A brilliant speaker and educator, Malcolm X became El-Hajj Malik El-Shabazz and gained a devoted following. He also made many enemies. He left the Nation of Islam and formed his own organization seeking black empowerment and human rights for all. He was assassinated in 1965 in Manhattan's Audubon Ballroom.

? Want to know more? Visit www.factsfornow.scholastic.com and enter the keywords **New York**.

PROTESTS AND PROGRESS

As the walls of segregation began to fall in the southern states in the 1960s, there was little improvement in the lives of northern African Americans. Many found no relief from low-paying jobs and inferior housing and schools. People began to lose hope. In 1964, this pent-up frustration exploded in riots in Rochester and Harlem. For the next five summers, urban America was torn by upheavals that burned down neighborhoods and left hundreds dead. But these explosions also focused the country on an old problem: discrimination in the land of the free. The result was the election of black mayors, government antipoverty programs, and the rise of a black power movement.

There were more protests, mainly focused on the Vietnam War. In 1965, demonstrations in New York City attracted 25,000 marchers against the war. At Columbia University in 1968, students occupied school buildings in an antiwar sit-in.

By the mid-1970s, New York's cities turned to economic issues and developed programs to bring new jobs and businesses to many cities. In Rochester, public schools were not meeting standards, but the city began an adopt-a-school program. Industry leaders successfully partnered with local schools to improve learning and reduce dropout rates.

Through the 1980s and 1990s, New York seemed to be surging forward. This prosperity mirrored the economic successes throughout the United States, brought about by the growth of technology industries.

Then came September 11, 2001. Terrorist attacks in New York City and Washington, D.C., stunned the nation and the world. Nearly 3,000 people died in New York City's World Trade Center. New Yorkers would never forget that day. To honor the memory of those who perished in the attack, the National September 11 Memorial & Museum was built on the site of the World Trade Center. The 8-acre (3.2 ha) memorial includes two pools, the walls of which are inscribed the names of each victim.

A memorial to the victims of September II, 200I, at a fire station in lower Manhattan

In late October 2012, Hurricane Sandy slammed into the East Coast of the United States. Nearly 150 people were killed, including about 50 in New York State. Total damages were estimated to be more than $68 billion. More than 650,000 homes and businesses were damaged or destroyed by flooding and fire. Large areas of New York City lost electricity for several days. Some seashore communities were completely wiped out, leaving thousands of residents homeless. New Yorkers quickly took up the task of rebuilding, and one year later, some areas had fully recovered. The complete process of rebuilding, however, may take decades.

READ ABOUT

New Yorkers and tourists alike enjoy walking through Bryant Park in New York City on a brisk spring day.

PEOPLE

★

N EW YORK STATE IS HOME TO
PEOPLE FROM NEARLY EVERY
CULTURE, EVERY NATION, AND
EVERY RELIGION. The state's 19 million people
are the very definition of the term *diversity*.
Some New Yorkers are from "the city," some
are from upstate, and some are from "the
island." But they pursue all the same jobs,
interests, and lifestyles as people throughout
the country. The Empire State has the third-
largest population in the United States, behind
California and Texas. Nearly half of all New
Yorkers live in New York City and its suburbs.

The Chinese New Year parade is one of many traditions upheld in Manhattan's Chinatown.

WORD TO KNOW

metropolitan *relating to a city and its surroundings*

PEOPLE FROM MANY LANDS

The New York **metropolitan** area, as defined by the U.S. Census, includes New York City, Westchester County to the north, Long Island to the east, and parts of Connecticut and New Jersey. Although the population totals in the millions, many residents in this area live in tight-knit neighborhoods. Stores, restaurants, and newspapers sold by street vendors reflect the ethnic backgrounds of the people who make up New York's diverse communities, regardless of whether they arrived in colonial times or two weeks ago.

In addition to the New York metropolitan area, there are five major urban areas along the Hudson-Erie Canal transportation route. They are Albany-Schnectady-Troy, Utica-Rome, Syracuse, Rochester, and Buffalo-Niagara Falls.

Where New Yorkers Live

The colors on this map indicate population density throughout the state. The darker the color, the more people live there.

People per square mile
- 10,000 or more
- 5,000 to 10,000
- 1,000 to 5,000
- 200 to 1,000
- 88 to 200
- 40 to 88
- 40 or fewer

Big City Life

This list shows the population of New York's biggest cities.

New York City	8,175,133
Buffalo	261,310
Rochester	210,565
Yonkers	195,976
Syracuse	145,170

Source: U.S. Census Bureau, 2010 census

People QuickFacts

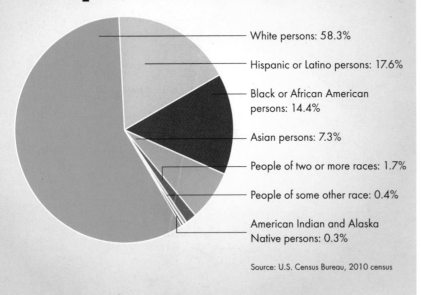

White persons: 58.3%

Hispanic or Latino persons: 17.6%

Black or African American persons: 14.4%

Asian persons: 7.3%

People of two or more races: 1.7%

People of some other race: 0.4%

American Indian and Alaska Native persons: 0.3%

Source: U.S. Census Bureau, 2010 census

Today, the majority of New Yorkers, 58.3 percent, are white. African Americans make up 14.4 percent of the state's population, or nearly 2.9 million people. Another 17.6 percent are of Hispanic heritage, and 7.3 percent are Asian.

Nearly 200,000 Native Americans live in the state, from Montauk Point to Niagara Falls. There are 10 federally recognized reservations in the state.

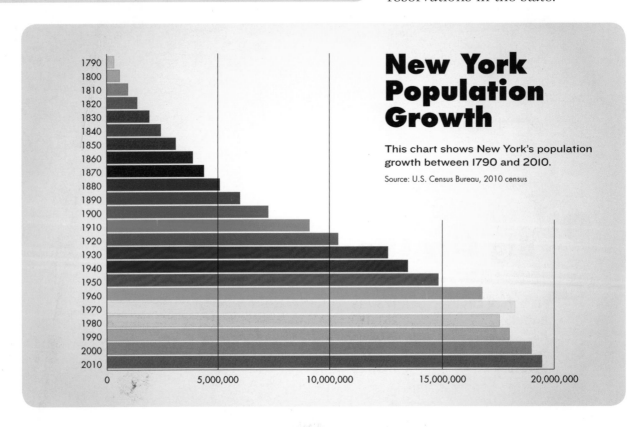

New York Population Growth

This chart shows New York's population growth between 1790 and 2010.

Source: U.S. Census Bureau, 2010 census

EDUCATION

New York puts a major emphasis on education, which consumes a large portion of the state's annual budget. Roughly 3.1 million students attend kindergarten through grade 12. Nearly 2.7 million students attend public schools, with about 390,000 students in private schools. School districts are run by boards of education, and board members are chosen by election within the district. Although it varies from district to district, state funds pay for about 35 percent of a school district's expenses, while taxes, federal aid, and other local revenue pay the remaining 65 percent. On average, New York State spends more than $17,000 for every student. Eighteen public schools in a variety of cities and towns throughout the state make the list of top 100 schools in the United States, according to *Newsweek* magazine.

High school students listen as their social studies teacher lectures about ancient Greek history.

Students practice the violin at the KIPP Academy in the South Bronx. KIPP stands for Knowledge Is Power Program, and this school has a respected music department.

SEE IT HERE!

CHAUTAUQUA INSTITUTION

In the 1800s, people in rural areas across the nation attended lectures in tents presented by the Chautauqua Institution in Chautauqua, New York. Today, lectures and programs continue to entertain and educate attendees about history, geography, and issues of current interest.

Every school district receives a "report card," just like its students. The report card measures school performance in English language arts, science, and math. The report cards give parents an idea where their school district ranks in relation to other districts and national standards.

School programs are based on core learning programs. Every New York student is exposed to language arts, foreign languages, social studies and history, math, science, technology, health, arts, and physical education. Before graduating from high school, students have to take and pass a number of standardized tests from the state Board of Regents.

At the university level, the State University of New York (SUNY) offers programs in all areas of pursuit. SUNY is a state-funded higher education program with 64 universities, community colleges, and technical schools. Tuition and costs are subsidized by state taxes. Older than the Brooklyn Bridge, SUNY Downstate was established as the Long Island College Hospital in 1860 and is the oldest school in the SUNY system. The SUNY system offers advanced programs—master's or doctorates—in a full range of subjects, including education, math, science, law, and medicine. New York is also home to a number of highly regarded private colleges and universities, including Cornell, Columbia, New York University, and Syracuse University.

THINK ABOUT IT!

Teach Cursive Writing?

PRO

Some people believe that cursive writing should no longer be taught in New York schools. They say few people use cursive in their day-to-day writing and instead rely on typing on keyboards. They argue that penmanship lessons should be limited to printing. This would give teachers time to focus on other skills and knowledge that would help students succeed.

CON

Other people say that cursive writing stimulates brain activity that printing does not. They claim writing in cursive leads to increased understanding. Some experts believe the speed and ease of writing in cursive allows students to focus more on what they are writing. Others would like to preserve the tradition of cursive writing, and argue that letters written in cursive tend to be saved and cherished, unlike e-mails.

HOW TO TALK LIKE A NEW YORKER

It isn't just what you say—but how you say it. There are some towns and cities in the state that only native New Yorkers seem to know how to pronounce. Here are some of them:

Albany: ALL-buh-nee
Madrid: MAA-drid
Oneonta: oh-nee-AHN-tuh
Poughkeepsie: puh-KIP-see
Chautauqua: chuh-TAW-kwa
Tonawanda: tah-nuh-WAHN-duh
Chappaqua: CHAP-puh-kwa
Ronkonkoma: rahn-KAHN-koh-muh
Massapequa: MASS-uh-PEE-kwa
Patchogue: PAA-chawg
Adirondacks: ad-ih-RAHN-daks
Quogue: KWAHG

HOW TO EAT LIKE A NEW YORKER

Order a submarine sandwich in New York and you'll get a 12-inch (30-cm) loaf of Italian bread stuffed with ham, salami, cheese, lettuce, tomato, garlic, and onion. Local bakeries provide fresh bagels and rolls, Italian cannoli, and other treats. The farms of New York offer big red apples, grapes, and corn on the cob. And coastal waters boast an abundance of seafood. See the opposite page—there's something for everyone.

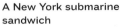
A New York submarine sandwich

MENU

WHAT'S ON THE MENU IN NEW YORK?

★ ★ ★

Beef-on-weck

In Buffalo, you'll find this specialty. It's thin-sliced roast beef on a hard roll called a *kummelweck* (coated with coarse salt and caraway seeds) and served with horseradish.

Buffalo wings

Named for their hometown, these are fried or grilled chicken wings in hot sauce.

Rice and beans (*arroz con frijoles*)

A standard in Spanish neighborhoods throughout New York. The spicier, the better.

Spiedies

When you're in Binghamton or Endicott, you'll find this treat (pronounced speed-ees): marinated meat, skewered and grilled.

Bagels with a schmeer and lox

Step into a deli and order this like a true New Yorker. It's a bagel with cream cheese and smoked salmon.

Reuben

What a sandwich! Grilled corned beef, sauerkraut, and Swiss cheese on rye.

Egg cream

A classic New York soda fountain drink made with milk, chocolate syrup, and seltzer.

Apple muffin

In 1987, students throughout the state banded together to get the apple muffin declared the official New York state muffin.

TRY THIS RECIPE
Waldorf Salad

This salad—featuring apples, the New York state fruit—was first served at Manhattan's Waldorf-Astoria Hotel. This is a low-fat version that tastes as good as the original recipe. Be sure to have an adult nearby to help.

Ingredients:
2 cups apples, peeled, cored, and diced into ½-inch cubes
¼ cup walnuts, chopped
¼ cup celery, ¼-inch slices
¼ cup raisins

Dressing:
½ cup plain yogurt
2 tablespoons honey
1 tablespoon lemon juice

Instructions:
Place apples, walnuts, celery, and raisins in a medium-sized bowl. Mix dressing ingredients in a small bowl. Pour the dressing over the apple mixture and toss. Serve chilled.

THE ART SCENE

New York has long been a center for the arts, entertainment, media, and sports. In the mid-19th century, artists of the Hudson River school painted stunning landscapes of the Hudson River. Among its best-known members were Thomas Cole, the movement's founder, and Asher Durand.

In the early 20th century, a group known as the Ashcan school depicted working-class lives in a realistic mode. Later in the 20th century, New York was home to such groundbreaking artists as Jackson Pollock, Roy Lichtenstein, Edward Hopper, Frank Stella, Helen Frankenthaler, Andy Warhol, and Kiki Smith.

New York City native Roy Lichtenstein poses with one of his pop-art paintings.

LITERATURE

The connection between New York State and literature stretches back to the early 1800s, when Washington Irving told tales of the colonial Dutch such as *Rip Van Winkle* and *The Legend of Sleepy Hollow.* In his Leatherstocking Tales, James Fenimore Cooper created the hero Natty Bumppo. His novel *Last of the Mohicans* (1826) was made into a feature film in 1992. In the 1920s, African American writers of the Harlem Renaissance drew portraits of the African American experience in novels such as Nella Larsen's *Passing* and poems like Claude McKay's "Harlem Dancer."

Young readers everywhere enjoy the writings of New York's Paula Danziger, Joseph Bruchac, and Maurice Sendak. *The Wonderful Wizard of Oz* is a classic by L. Frank Baum, who was born in Chittenango. New York City–born Julia Alvarez, winner of the Americas Award for *Before We Were Free*, wrote *In the Time of Butterflies* about girls growing up in the Dominican Republic under a dictatorship. She is also the author of *How the Garcia Girls Lost Their Accents.*

ON STAGE AND SCREEN

Music fills the air throughout New York State. Every flavor of recorded music can be heard on radio

MINI-BIO

JOSEPH BRUCHAC: STORYTELLER

Joseph Bruchac (1942–) grew up in a small town in the foothills of the Adirondacks. His grandfather was Abenaki, and Bruchac's ties to Native American culture appear in many of his books. Although he never heard Indian stories from his grandfather, he sought out other native elders. His first book of stories was published in 1975. Among Bruchac's many published works are *A Boy Called Slow: The True Story of Sitting Bull; Crazy Horse's Vision;* and *The Arrow over the Door.*

? Want to know more? Visit www.factsfornow .scholastic.com and enter the keywords **New York**.

MINI-BIO

JAY-Z: RAPPER AND BUSINESSPERSON

Jay-Z (1969–) was born Shawn Corey Carter in Brooklyn. He grew up in a rough neighborhood, and turned to rap to escape the violence and poverty that surrounded him. In the late 1990s, he began to release a string of number one albums and hit singles. Jay-Z soon branched out into other enterprises, starting a popular line of clothing and a film company. In 2008, he married singer and songwriter Beyoncé Knowles.

? **Want to know more?** Visit www.factsfornow .scholastic.com and enter the keywords **New York**.

stations from western New York to the eastern tip of Long Island. Every major city has a symphony, a dance company, and active musical theater.

New York was the birthplace of many well-known musicians, as well as musical styles. Tony Bennett, Billy Joel, Alicia Keys, Jennifer Lopez, and Mariah Carey are all New York natives. And New

Street musicians entertaining a crowd in a churchyard in New York City

York City was the birthplace of hip-hop and some of its better-known artists, including LL Cool J, Run-D.M.C., Jay-Z, and Sean Combs, aka Diddy and Puff Daddy. Tito Puente was a talented Latin jazz musician and bandleader. He was born in Spanish Harlem and studied at the Juilliard School of Music.

In the theater, award-winning writer Neil Simon portrayed his home state in plays such as *The Odd Couple*. Pulitzer Prize—winner Arthur Miller was born in New York. He penned the classic *Death of a Salesman*.

New Yorker Wendy Wasserstein received the 1989 Tony Award, Pulitzer Prize, and Drama Desk award for *The Heidi Chronicles*. She began a program in 1998 called Open Doors to take underprivileged New York high school students to the theater.

When you go to the movies or watch TV, you're bound to see lots of New Yorkers on the screen. Claire Danes was born in New York City, as was Sarah Michelle Gellar. Actor Denzel Washington hails from Mount Vernon, and actor Cuba Gooding Jr. was born in the Bronx. Actor Adam Sandler was born in Brooklyn and graduated from New York University. Have you ever watched reruns of *The Twilight Zone* TV show? Creator and narrator Rod Serling was born in Syracuse and grew up in Binghamton.

MINI-BIO

YO-YO MA: GENIUS ON THE CELLO

Born in Paris, France, to Chinese parents, Yo-Yo Ma (1955–) came to New York when he was seven. He had begun playing the cello when he was four, and at age eight, he was in a TV concert conducted by the acclaimed Leonard Bernstein. He studied at the Juilliard School of Music, Columbia University, and Harvard University. Today, Yo-Yo Ma is considered one of the finest cellists in the world. But he is also appreciated for making classical music appealing to everyone. He a winner of multiple Grammy Awards, and he was named a UN peace ambassador in 2006.

? **Want to know more?** Visit www.factsfornow .scholastic.com and enter the keywords **New York**.

GOOD SPORTS

From one end of the state to the other, New Yorkers are avid sports enthusiasts. "Take Me Out to the Ball Game" isn't just a song in New York—it's a lifestyle.

The state boasts professional teams in a wide range of sports. The Buffalo Bills have a long history in football. So do the New York Giants and the New York Jets, who technically play in New Jersey at the Meadowlands. The latter two football teams have die-hard fans in both states. The 1990 Super Bowl was a New York classic, with the Giants facing the Buffalo Bills. The Giants won 20–19.

The New York Knicks shoot hoops at Madison Square Garden, and a popular commentator is Walt "Clyde" Frazier, a former star of the team. The Knicks won the NBA championship in 1970 and 1973. The

Quarterback Eli Manning calls a play for the New York Giants in a 2012 game against the New York Jets.

New York Liberty guard Cappie Pondexter drives toward the basket in a 2013 game against the Chicago Sky.

women of the New York Liberty have been wowing basketball fans since the WNBA was founded in 1997.

On the ice, New York has three hockey teams: the Buffalo Sabres, the New York Rangers, and the New York Islanders. The Rangers and the Islanders have each won the Stanley Cup four times.

New York baseball fans root for the Yankees, who play in the Bronx, or the Mets, who play in Queens. Both teams have been powerhouses for decades. The Yankees have won the World Series a record 27 times, and the Mets have captured that championship twice. They even played each other in 2000 in what was called the Subway Series.

The Empire State has produced some remarkable athletes. Baseball legend Lou Gehrig was born in New York City and played for the Yankees his entire career,

In 1947, Jackie Robinson (#42) opened the door for African Americans to enter professional baseball. Here he scores the wining run against the Chicago Cubs at Ebbets Field.

FAQ ★ ★ ★

Q8 WHO WAS JACKIE ROBINSON?

A8 Some historians say segregation was first defeated on April 15, 1947, at Ebbets Field, Brooklyn. Wearing Dodger uniform #42, a rookie named Jackie Robinson picked up his infielder's glove and trotted onto the diamond. Robinson not only broke baseball's color line that day, but his heroism (and his hitting, running, and fielding) began to topple segregation in sports and start its collapse in the United States.

from 1923 to 1939. Known as the Iron Horse, Gehrig played 2,130 consecutive games, a record that he held until 1995, when it was broken by Cal Ripken. Gehrig retired from the game when he was diagnosed with a muscular disease called ALS, now often called Lou Gehrig's disease.

Another baseball player who made his mark in New York was Jackie Robinson. He was the first African American to play major league baseball. He broke the color barrier in 1947 and played with the Brooklyn Dodgers (before they moved to Los Angeles) until 1956.

Tennis great John McEnroe was born in Germany, but he and his brother Patrick grew up in Douglaston. These days, you can hear both of them as commentators for the game.

Born in Harlem as Lou Alcindor, Kareem Abdul-Jabar led Power Memorial High School to three New York City basketball championships. He went on to be

MINI-BIO

LIA NEAL: OLYMPIC SWIMMER

Lia Neal (1995—) was born and raised in Brooklyn, New York. She is the daughter of a Chinese American mother and an African American father. Lia began swimming at the age of six. She developed into a fast and powerful swimmer, and was soon on her way to international competition. In the 2011 World Junior Championships, Lia won a gold medal in the 100-meter freestyle and a silver medal in the 50-meter freestyle events. At the 2012 Olympic Games in London, England, she won a bronze medal with her three teammates in the 4x100-meter freestyle relay.

? Want to know more? Visit www.factsfornow .scholastic.com and enter the keywords **New York**.

a star at UCLA and played professionally for the Milwaukee Bucks (1969 to 1975) and the Los Angeles Lakers (1975 to 1989). He still holds the records for the most points scored in NBA history and the most minutes played.

Ice-skating sisters Sarah and Emily Hughes are from Great Neck, Long Island. Sarah Hughes won the gold medal at the 2002 Winter Olympics.

No matter what the season, New Yorkers love to both watch and play sports. They are great fans and great competitors, too.

Long Island native Sarah Hughes competing in the women's free skate program at the 2002 Winter Olympics in Salt Lake City

READ ABOUT

Members of the New York State General Assembly debate bills during a session at the state capitol in Albany.

CHAPTER SEVEN

GOVERNMENT

★

G OVERNING NEW YORK IS LIKE GOVERNING A SMALL COUNTRY. The state budget is more than $130 billion, which is larger than the national budgets of many countries! New York's population is larger than the combined populations of Austria and Switzerland. It takes a large, efficient government to deal with the needs and welfare of more than 19 million people.

Capitol Facts

Here are some fascinating facts about New York's state capitol.

Years of construction: 1867–1889

Height: 220 feet (67 m)

Length: 400 feet (122 m)

Width: 2,300 feet (701 m)

Number of floors: 5, with full basement and attic

Location: Empire State Plaza, Albany

Architects: Thomas Fuller, later replaced by Leopold Eidlitz and Henry Hobson Richardson

Construction material: Gray granite

Outstanding feature: The Million Dollar Staircase, lined with more than 300 carved portraits of famous New Yorkers and others

WHERE IT ALL HAPPENS

The state's government is set up by its constitution. The original version of this document was drafted by John Jay, who went on to serve as chief justice of the U.S. Supreme Court. And it was adopted in Kingston, the state's first capital, on April 20, 1777. Today, the capital of New York is located in Albany.

As with all states, the government is divided into three branches: executive, legislative, and judicial. The powers of each branch are designed to balance out the powers of the others.

The state capitol in Albany

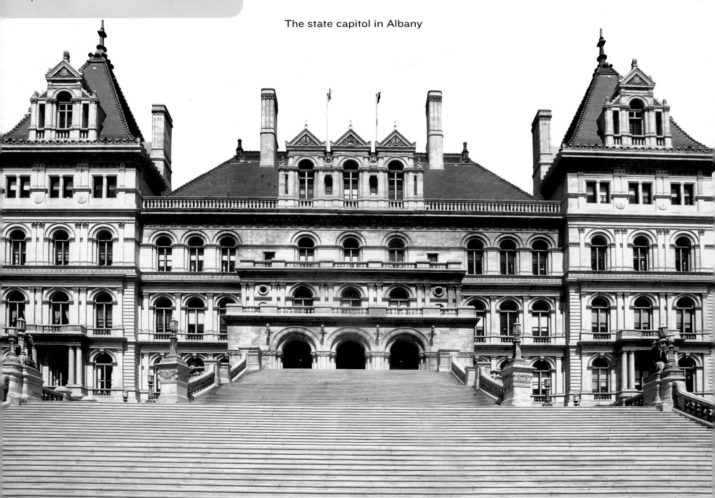

Capital City

This map shows places of interest around Albany, New York's capital city.

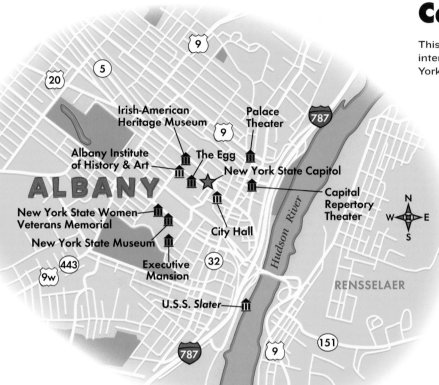

THE EXECUTIVE BRANCH

The head of the executive branch is the governor. In New York, the governor is in charge of carrying out the laws of the state. There are many departments in the executive branch, a number determined by the state's constitution. Typical executive departments include budgeting, central purchasing, state police, and education.

In an election, the governor and lieutenant governor are on a shared ballot. This means that voters cannot, for example, choose a Republican governor and a Democratic lieutenant governor. A governor serves for four years with no term limits, so if the people choose, a person could be governor 20, 32, or even 40 consecutive years.

SEE IT HERE!

THE EXECUTIVE MANSION

New York's governor lives in the Executive Mansion, located on Eagle Street in downtown Albany. A journey through the mansion takes visitors from the 1800s to the present. On one of the special tours designed for school classes, students learn about governors and first ladies, issues that faced the state, and the culture of New York. Furniture, artifacts, and art give an accurate idea about how governors have lived in the past.

New York's State Government

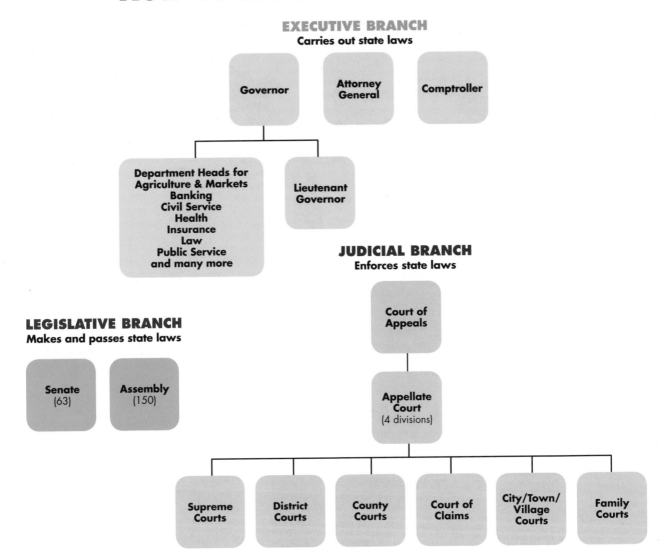

EXECUTIVE BRANCH
Carries out state laws

Governor

Attorney General

Comptroller

Department Heads for
Agriculture & Markets
Banking
Civil Service
Health
Insurance
Law
Public Service
and many more

Lieutenant Governor

JUDICIAL BRANCH
Enforces state laws

Court of Appeals

Appellate Court
(4 divisions)

Supreme Courts

District Courts

County Courts

Court of Claims

City/Town/Village Courts

Family Courts

LEGISLATIVE BRANCH
Makes and passes state laws

Senate
(63)

Assembly
(150)

Four former New York governors were chosen as president of the United States: Martin Van Buren, Grover Cleveland, Theodore Roosevelt, and Franklin D. Roosevelt.

The governor's closest advisers form a cabinet. New York's executive cabinet is larger than any other state's. Even California, with a larger population, has a smaller cabinet. The governor appoints most cabinet officials, although New Yorkers elect the comptroller (much like a treasurer) and the attorney general (the state's primary lawyer).

THE LEGISLATIVE BRANCH

The New York legislature began in 1777. That was 12 years before the U.S. Constitution established the U.S. Congress. The legislative branch has two divisions: the senate and the assembly. Both groups have equal lawmaking powers and responsibilities.

The New York senate has 63 members, one for each district; districts correspond to the number of counties in the state. In addition to proposing new laws or changes to the state constitution, the senate confirms people appointed by the governor. Typical appointments that the senate reviews are justices and cabinet officials. Although not a member of the senate, the lieutenant governor serves as the president of the senate and can vote if the senators' votes on a measure end up in a tie.

The assembly consists of 150 members. They each represent approximately 120,000 people. Both senators and assembly members serve two-year terms and can be reelected for an unlimited number of terms. Every year, thousands of bills are proposed in the assembly, but usually only 4 to 5 percent of them are passed. For a bill to become a law, it must pass by a simple majority in each house and then be signed by the governor.

MINI-BIO

GEORGE CLINTON: NEW YORK'S FIRST GOVERNOR

George Clinton (1739–1812) was New York State's first governor and its longest-serving governor in history. As a young man, Clinton enlisted in the British army to fight in the French and Indian War (1754–1763). He later became a lawyer and was elected to the Continental Congress. He served as the governor of New York from 1777 to 1795, and again from 1801 to 1804. He was also vice president of the United States under Thomas Jefferson and James Madison.

? **Want to know more?** Visit www.factsfornow.scholastic.com and enter the keywords **New York**.

New York was the first state to require license plates on cars.

Representing New York

This list shows the number of elected officials who represent New York, both on the state and national levels.

OFFICE	NUMBER	LENGTH OF TERM
State senators	63	2 years
State assembly members	150	2 years
U.S. senators	2	6 years
U.S. representatives	27	2 years
Presidential electors	29	—

In 1994, New York State passed a law requiring helmets for all bikers, skateboarders, and in-line skaters up to age 14.

Out of concern for the well-being of its children, the state legislature has passed a number of laws that deal with child safety. New York's seat-belt laws declare that children under 16 must be restrained when riding in cars. Fines for failure to buckle up are $50. If the offense takes place in the front seat, the driver can also be fined. This law also goes for school buses. All buses built after July 1, 1987, must be equipped with child safety belts.

In addition to seat belts, New York requires that all bikers, in-line skaters up to 14 years old, scooter riders, and skateboarders must wear helmets.

Bikes must have brakes, a horn or bell, and both head-lights and taillights if ridden after dark. In addition, the bikes must have reflective tires or spoke-mounted reflectors. The state insists that manufacturers equip skates with a type of brake and recommend protective gear.

New Yorkers have all the freedoms guaranteed under the U.S. Constitution and a host of laws that control how those freedoms are used. Although some of these laws may seem confining, such as insisting on helmets for scooter riders, they are passed for the benefit of the state's citizens.

THE JUDICIAL BRANCH

New York's justice system is not laid out like most other states. The highest court in New York is the court of appeals. The court consists of a chief judge and six associate judges, all appointed to 14-year terms by the governor. In simple terms, the court of appeals has the final say about issues of law in the state.

The New York Supreme Court is not "supreme" at all. That is to say, it is not the topmost or upper court. Covering both civil and criminal cases, the supreme court is the trial court of New York. The justices, who preside over the supreme court, hear civil cases such as a lawsuit against a company or person and criminal cases that deal with theft, murder, or fraud.

WORKING FOR THE PEOPLE

New York's statewide family court oversees the welfare of children. The court administers child protective services, ensures that child support is paid in divorce situations, and finalizes adoptions. The court also works with children who have committed crimes. It oversees juvenile detention centers and **probation** for child offenders.

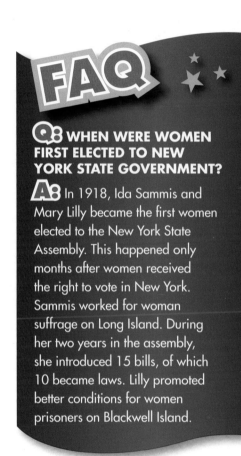

FAQ

Q: WHEN WERE WOMEN FIRST ELECTED TO NEW YORK STATE GOVERNMENT?

A: In 1918, Ida Sammis and Mary Lilly became the first women elected to the New York State Assembly. This happened only months after women received the right to vote in New York. Sammis worked for woman suffrage on Long Island. During her two years in the assembly, she introduced 15 bills, of which 10 became laws. Lilly promoted better conditions for women prisoners on Blackwell Island.

WORD TO KNOW

probation *a time during which a person convicted of a crime is evaluated*

New York Counties

This map shows the 62 counties in New York. Albany, the state capital, is indicated with a star.

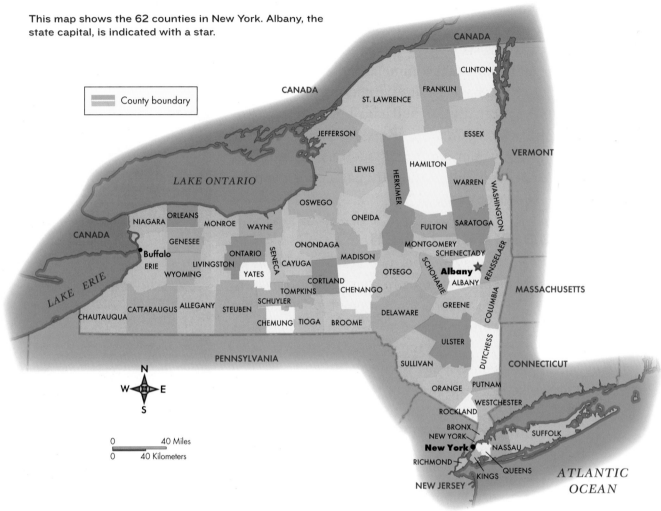

LOCAL GOVERNMENT

Throughout the state of New York, local governments keep the towns and cities working. Each of the 62 counties has its own court. And towns elect leaders who look out for the interests of their people. These councils pass laws about social services. They help keep police departments and public libraries running.

MINI-BIO

ELEANOR ROOSEVELT: THE NATION'S SOCIAL CONSCIENCE

When *Time* magazine listed its 100 most influential people of the 20th century, Eleanor Roosevelt (1884–1962) was one of 18 women and the only first lady on the list. Roosevelt was born in New York City. As first lady, she became the social conscience of the nation, speaking out for the rights of women, minorities, and children.

During World War II, she worked tirelessly for the American cause, visiting sick and wounded servicemen and troops behind the battlefront. After the death of her husband, President Franklin D. Roosevelt, Eleanor thought her public life was over. However, she became the first U.S. ambassador to the United Nations.

❓ Want to know more? Visit www.factsfornow .scholastic.com and enter the keywords **New York**.

WORLD LEADERS

In addition to being a world economic leader, New York has also produced diplomats, ambassadors, and world political leaders. Supreme Court chief justice John Roberts Jr. hails from Buffalo. Supreme Court justices Ruth Bader Ginsburg, Elena Kagan, and Sonia Sotomayor were all born in New York City. Five New Yorkers have become U.S. presidents, and 11 have become vice presidents.

U.S. PRESIDENTS FROM NEW YORK

Grover Cleveland (1837–1908) was born in New Jersey, but spent much of his childhood and adult life in New York. He worked as a lawyer, Erie County sheriff, mayor of Buffalo, and New York governor. Cleveland is the only president who served two nonconsecutive terms (1885–1889; and 1893–1897).

Millard Fillmore (1800–1874) was the 13th president of the United States. Born in Summerhill, Fillmore struggled to get an education and succeeded in becoming a lawyer in 1828. He was later elected to the New York legislature. A member of the Whig Party, Fillmore took office as vice president in 1849. A year later, he became president when Zachary Taylor died in office.

Franklin D. Roosevelt (1882–1945) became president during the Great Depression. During his first 100 days in office, he proposed programs to get America back to work through the Works Progress Administration, the Tennessee Valley Authority program, the Civilian Conservation Corps, and dozens of other aggressive government programs. The only president to serve four terms, FDR saw the country through the Depression.

Theodore Roosevelt (1858–1919) was a rugged outdoorsman who hunted, fished, and enjoyed the American West. He became president when William McKinley was assassinated in 1901. He served as president from 1901 to 1909 and is best known for establishing the national parks program. The teddy bear is named after Teddy Roosevelt.

Martin Van Buren (1782–1862) was called the Little Magician and the Red Fox of Kinderhook. Born in Kinderhook in the Hudson River valley, Van Buren was a lawyer and governor of New York before becoming president in 1837.

State Flag

New York's state flag features the state coat of arms against a dark blue field, with the goddesses Liberty and Justice on either side. The official flag was adopted in 1901.

State Seal

The current version of the state seal was last modified in 1882 to depict New York State's commitment to liberty and justice, its enduring optimism, and its faith in the strength of the human spirit.

Two goddesses are featured on the seal. Liberty stands with a crown at her feet. Her position over the crown symbolizes the American colonies' victory in the Revolutionary War. Justice is blindfolded and holds the scales of justice. This means that all citizens, regardless of class or color, are entitled to equal treatment under the law. In the center shield, ships of commerce sail the Hudson River as the sun rises over the Hudson Highlands. On top is an eagle resting on a globe. This represents New York's place in the Western Hemisphere. A banner has the state motto, *Excelsior*, meaning "Ever Upward."

READ ABOUT

A tug-boat alongside
a freight ship in New
York Harbor

CHAPTER EIGHT

ECONOMY

★

IF NEW YORK WERE A NATION ON ITS OWN, ITS ECONOMY WOULD RANK 15TH IN THE WORLD, SLIGHTLY SMALLER THAN CANADA OR SPAIN. In 2010, New York's gross state product, the value of all products and services produced in the state, totaled more than $1.1 trillion. Among states, New York is third in economic productivity, behind California and Texas.

THE TRANSPORTATION NETWORK

One reason New York's economy has flourished is the abundance of available transportation. A network of roads throughout the state and connecting with other states and Canada make truck shipping quick. New York City has a bustling deepwater seaport, with container ships moving in and out on a jam-packed schedule. LaGuardia and John F. Kennedy airports are two of the busiest in the United States, and there are smaller airports in all major New York cities. New York City is a central hub for train traffic as well, with commuter and freight trains moving through Grand Central and Penn stations. Within New York City, subways and buses move on a 24-hour, seven-days-a-week schedule. Buffalo has a light-rail service.

All this transportation provides avenues for bringing in New York's major imports—rough diamonds, gold, aluminum, natural gas, electricity, and lumber. The diamonds are cut in New York City's diamond district and become a valuable export as cut diamonds. The state also exports foodstuffs (dairy, meat, fruit, and vegetables), minerals, and auto parts. Although New York trades with many nations, its primary foreign business partner is Canada.

BUSINESS AND INDUSTRY

In recent years, the Empire State has undergone major changes in business and industry. Overall, there is a trend toward deindustrialization, with new types of businesses developing statewide. Major international companies such as Eastman Kodak, Xerox, and IBM have scaled down their large upstate operations and now maintain only smaller facilities. Trico, a company that developed the first windshield wiper and was once

the largest employer in Buffalo, totally closed down its plant there in 1998.

New businesses, however, are quickly replacing traditional New York industries. GlobalFoundries, the world's second-largest maker of computer chips, operates a huge facility in Saratoga County. The company plans to build a second factory, which will increase its total number of employees to nearly 7,000.

Small Internet-based companies are also part of the state's new economy. Hundreds of start-ups operate in New York City, offering unique products and services to people around the world. Once a major manufacturing center, New York City now is more likely to provide services than manufacture goods. The primary money-makers in New York City are finance, insurance, and real estate.

These IBM employees work in a Fishkill, New York, plant that makes computer chips.

New York City's Federal Reserve Bank has the largest gold storage in the world—larger than Fort Knox! The vault lies 80 feet (24 m) below street level and holds $90 billion worth of gold.

WORD TO KNOW

stock *a monetary investment in a company*

The world of finance includes banking, money loans, and the purchase and sale of **stock**. The world center for finance is Wall Street in New York City. The New York Stock Exchange is the world's largest market for buying and selling stocks, bonds, and mutual funds. The NASDAQ (National Association of Securities Dealers Automated Quotations), the third-largest stock exchange, is also a New York City operation. Buying and selling stocks, advising people about what stocks and bonds to purchase, and handling the money is a multibillion-dollar-a-day business.

New York City is also known for fashion, advertising, publishing, media, and medical research. The fashion industry is centered in the garment district, although much of the manufacture of clothes is now done overseas. The focal point of U.S. advertising is Madison Avenue, but agencies are spread throughout the city. Many of the print ads that appear in magazines and television commercials nationwide are designed, written, and produced by New York City's many ad agencies.

Many book-publishing companies are headquartered in Manhattan. Authors may write anywhere, but when it comes to publishing books, New York City is the place to be. The publishing industry also includes newspapers. Hundreds of newspapers and magazines have offices in New York.

MINI-BIO

VERA WANG: NEW YORK FASHIONISTA

Vera Wang (1949–) is a native New Yorker and brilliant fashion designer, but did you know she was once a talented figure skater? Wang competed at the national level in figure skating pairs and came in fifth in the U.S. junior pairs in 1969. After earning her art degree, she began working for Vogue magazine. Following that, she designed accessories for Ralph Lauren. She is probably known best for designing wedding gowns.

In 2005, Wang was named womenswear designer of the year by the Council of Fashion Designers of America.

? **Want to know more?** Visit www.factsfornow .scholastic.com and enter the keywords **New York**.

MIKE LUPICA: NEWSPAPER COLUMNIST

Mike Lupica (1952–), born in Oneida, began his newspaper career at age 23 covering the New York Knicks basketball team for the New York Post. He joined the New York Daily News in 1997, where he currently writes his popular Shooting from the Lip column, which appears every Sunday. Lupica has also written sports biographies, magazine articles, and novels for adults and young adults, some which have become national best sellers. He frequently appears on ESPN sports shows and is often a guest on television news programs.

? **Want to know more?** Visit www.factsfornow.scholastic.com and enter the keywords **New York**.

Newspapers in New York are published in a wide range of languages and appeal to people from many different cultural backgrounds.

Many news broadcasts, television shows, and soap operas are produced in New York studios. Radio stations cater to every possible listening audience: classical, rock, gospel, jazz, news/talk, sports, pop, and Caribbean—in English, Spanish, Mandarin Chinese, Korean, and Russian.

New York is a leader in the areas of health care and medical research. The University of Buffalo is a center for cutting-edge research in cardiac care. The Roswell Park Cancer Institute in Buffalo offers educational programs for talented high school students interested in careers in medicine or medical research. New York City boasts dozens of hospitals and thousands of doctors.

GETTING THE NEWS

El Diario/La Prensa ("The Journal/The Press") is the oldest Spanish-language newspaper in the country and the largest one in New York City. It was established in 1963 when *El Diario de Nueva York* (dating from 1947) and *La Prensa* (dating from 1913) merged. It covers local, national, and international news, and focuses on Latino interests. Each day, almost 300,000 people read the paper.

What Do New Yorkers Do?

This color-coded chart shows what industries New Yorkers work in.

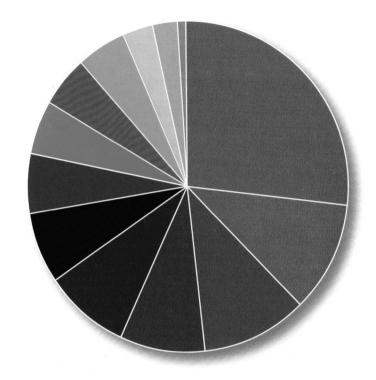

27.0% Educational services, and health care and social assistance, 2,443,001

10.9% Professional, scientific, and management, and administrative and waste management services, 985,821

10.6% Retail trade, 963,903

8.6% Arts, entertainment, and recreation, and accommodation and food services, 779,398

8.5% Finance and insurance, and real estate and rental and leasing, 765,322

7.1% Manufacturing, 638,955

5.8% Construction, 524,793

5.3% Transportation and warehousing, and utilities, 476,450

5.0% Other services, except public administration, 456,955

4.9% Public administration, 446,255

3.0% Information, 274,349

2.7% Wholesale trade, 241,660

0.6% Agriculture, forestry, fishing and hunting, and mining, 54,806

Source: U.S. Census Bureau, 2010 census

WOW

The first cattle ranch in the United States was started in 1747 at Montauk, Long Island. Still in business today, it is now known as the Deep Hollow Ranch.

AGRICULTURE

Twenty percent of New York's land is involved in some type of agriculture. That's roughly 7 million acres (2.8 million ha) and 36,000 farms. The state is a major dairy producer, ranking fourth in the nation in the production of milk, butter, yogurt, and cheese. Cattle, hog, and sheep farms provide beef, pork, mutton, and lamb. New York produces eggs, ducks, chickens, and turkeys.

Annually, New York harvests roughly $325 million worth of fruit, largely depending upon weather. The state is second in the United States in apples and third in grapes. Pears and strawberries are also grown there.

Thriving vegetable farms in New York grow cabbage, sweet corn, and onions. New York potatoes, tomatoes, pumpkins, cucumbers, squash, green peas, and cauliflower find their way to supermarkets throughout the Northeast and beyond. New York ranks second behind Vermont in volume of maple syrup produced.

Few people think of flowers when they think of New York, but the state's floriculture market passes its fruit production—$400 million yearly. Most of the floriculture products are seedlings, potted plants, and shrubs, along with a reasonably strong market in Christmas trees.

NATURAL RESOURCES

Nearly 90 percent of New York's mining operations produce sand, gravel, and limestone. Crushed gravel or rock is used in concrete, blacktop, road fill, and construction. The state also mines a number of industrial products.

SEE IT HERE!

THE OLD CHATHAM SHEEPHERDING COMPANY

If you've never seen sheep being milked—and few people have—the Old Chatham Sheepherding Company is a must-see. Located in the Hudson Valley, this 1,200-sheep farm is the largest sheep dairy in the country, producing top-quality yogurt, ricotta cheese, and a delicious Hudson Valley Camembert cheese.

THE FABULOUS CHEWING GUM ACCIDENT

The invention of chewing gum began with ousted Mexican president Santa Ana and a plan to make rubber. Santa Ana was staying with the Adams family on Staten Island in the late 1800s, and he suggested that Thomas Adams find a way to blend chicle (the sap of the sapodilla tree) with rubber to make tires. The idea bombed, but the resulting product was a gum that could be chewed. And that was that! The Adams family began producing chewing gum, and they sold it with the slogan "Adams New York Gum No. 1— Snapping and Stretching." It may not be a catchy phrase, but chewing gum made the Adams family a fortune.

Major Agricultural and Mining Products

This map shows where New York's major agricultural and mining products come from. See a cow? That means cattle are raised there.

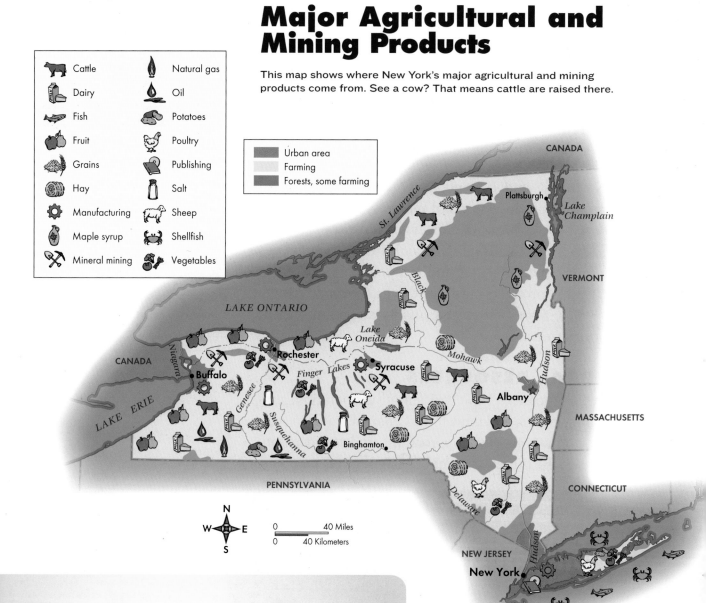

Legend:

Cattle		Natural gas	
Dairy		Oil	
Fish		Potatoes	
Fruit		Poultry	
Grains		Publishing	
Hay		Salt	
Manufacturing		Sheep	
Maple syrup		Shellfish	
Mineral mining		Vegetables	

Urban area
Farming
Forests, some farming

Top Products

Agriculture Milk and dairy products, apples, grapes, maple syrup, cabbage, sweet corn, onions, hay

Livestock Cattle, hogs, sheep and lambs, eggs, ducks, broilers, turkeys

Mining Limestone, emery, garnet, talc, salt, sand, gravel, wollastonite

New York gypsum is used to make cement, plaster, and wallboard for building. Garnet is the most popular substance for blast cleaning, also called sandblasting, and is also used as the grit on fine or coarse sandpaper.

Two products—emery and wollastonite—are New York state exclusives. No other state has quantities of these minerals. Emery is used to make nail files and industrial abrasives, while wollastonite is commonly used in making paints, plastics, and ceramics. New York ranks third in the nation in mining salt.

Natural resources in New York include seafood and fish. Some freshwater commercial fishing takes place on Lakes Erie and Ontario. However, the state's seafood industry is centered on Long Island. Fishing vessels head out from Montauk Point to catch bluefin tuna and bass. Closer to shore, catches include flounder, squid, clams, and lobsters.

From Upstate New York to Manhattan, the state is brimming with great ideas and unique businesses. Its fields produce bountiful harvests, and its boardrooms produce remarkable products and services. All this innovation makes New York an astounding place!

New York's state gem, the garnet

NEW YORK AND #2 PENCILS

Have you ever used a Ticonderoga #2 pencil? For many years, a mine near Ticonderoga, New York, produced quality graphite that makes up the "lead" in #2 soft pencils. The brand name, Ticonderoga, originally indicated pencils made with New York graphite.

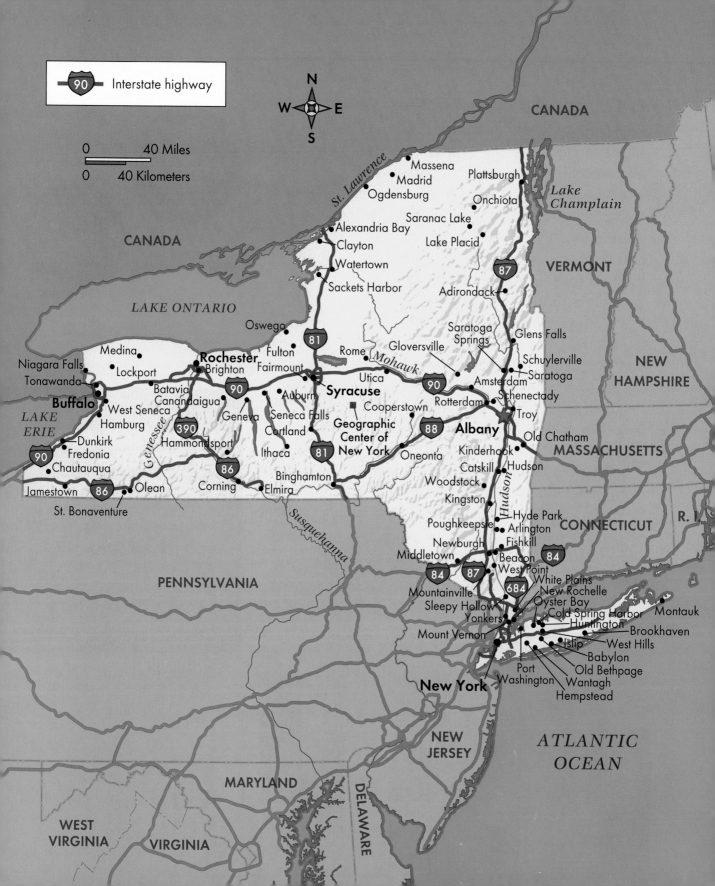

Interstate highway 90

N
W · E
S

0   40 Miles
0   40 Kilometers

CANADA

CANADA

St. Lawrence

Massena
Madrid
Ogdensburg
Plattsburgh
Onchiota
Saranac Lake
Lake Placid
Alexandria Bay
Clayton
Watertown
Sackets Harbor
Adirondack

Lake Champlain

VERMONT

87

LAKE ONTARIO

Oswego

Medina
Lockport
Rochester
Brighton
Fulton
Fairmount
Rome
Mohawk
Gloversville
Saratoga Springs
Glens Falls
Schuylerville
Saratoga

NEW HAMPSHIRE

Niagara Falls
Tonawanda
Batavia
Canandaigua
90
Auburn
Utica
Syracuse
90
Amsterdam
Schenectady

Buffalo
West Seneca
Hamburg
390
Geneva
Seneca Falls
Cortland
Cooperstown
Rotterdam
Troy
Old Chatham

LAKE ERIE
Dunkirk
Fredonia
Chautauqua
Hammondsport
Ithaca
Geographic Center of New York
88
Albany
Kinderhook
MASSACHUSETTS

Jamestown
86
Olean
86
Corning
Elmira
Binghamton
81
Oneonta
Catskill
Hudson
Woodstock
Kingston

St. Bonaventure

Genessee

Susquehanna

PENNSYLVANIA

Hyde Park
Arlington
Fishkill
CONNECTICUT
R. I.

Hudson

84

Newburgh
Middletown
Beacon
West Point
White Plains
New Rochelle
Oyster Bay
Cold Spring Harbor
Huntington
Montauk
Brookhaven
West Hills
Babylon
Old Bethpage
Port Washington
Wantagh
Hempstead

84
87
684

Mountainville
Sleepy Hollow
Yonkers
Mount Vernon
Islip

New York

NEW JERSEY

ATLANTIC OCEAN

MARYLAND

DELAWARE

WEST VIRGINIA

VIRGINIA

CHAPTER NINE

TRAVEL GUIDE

★

PERHAPS YOU'VE SEEN THE BUMPER STICKERS WITH THE SLOGAN "I ♥ NY." The people of New York love to hike and swim. They love to visit museums and art galleries. They love the small towns and the big cities. With so much to see and do here, it's hard not to love this state. So grab your map, and let's go.

MAINE

← Follow along with this travel map. We'll begin in Buffalo and travel up and around to New York City!

CHAUTAUQUA ALLEGHENY/ GREATER NIAGARA REGION

THINGS TO DO: Take a misty boat tour of Niagara Falls, visit a carousel factory, tour an art museum, or stroll through a historic community.

Buffalo

★ **Buffalo Museum of Science:** With dozens of exhibits covering millions of years of natural history and science, the Buffalo Museum of Science in Humboldt Park is a great geological museum, and a fun place to spend an afternoon.

★ **Herschell Carrousel Factory Museum:** The historical museum in Delaware Park features the history of carousel making, carving demonstrations, and a historic operating carousel.

★ **Ralph Wilson Stadium:** Grab a blanket, and watch exciting NFL action at Ralph Wilson Stadium, home of the Buffalo Bills.

Niagara Falls

★ **Niagara Falls:** The famous waterfalls were formed 10,000 years ago and are considered a natural wonder. Each minute the Niagara River spills 40 million gallons (151 million liters) of water 180 feet (55 m) downward across a ragged ledge nearly two-thirds of a mile (1 km) wide.

★ **Niagara Wax Museum of History:** The history of Greater Niagara is depicted with life-sized wax figures. A fun-filled experience for everyone.

Chautauqua

★ **Chautauqua Institution:** Founded in 1874, this National Historic Landmark offers studies in theater, music, arts, religion, and the pursuit of knowledge.

Niagara Falls

Chautauqua Institution

St. Bonaventure

★ **Regina A. Quick Center for the Arts:** This arts center features contemporary and historic European and American art, as well as Asian, Greek, and Southwestern ceramics.

FINGER LAKES REGION

THINGS TO DO: Learn about the Erie Canal, tour historic homes, or discover the world of photography.

Rochester

★ **Susan B. Anthony House:** This was the home of woman suffrage movement leader Susan B. Anthony, and the site of her arrest for voting in 1872. This National Historic site features exhibits on the woman suffrage movement. Also, don't miss the "Let's Have Tea" statue of Anthony and Frederick Douglass located adjacent to the property.

★ **George Eastman House:** Walk through the mansion and gardens of Eastman Kodak Company founder George Eastman. This National Historic Site features a museum on the history and innovation of photography and motion pictures.

★ **Rochester Museum & Science Center/Strasenburgh Planetarium:** Immerse yourself in three floors of interactive exhibits on science and technology, the region's cultural heritage, and natural environment. Also, be sure to check out the four-story-high planetarium dome!

Syracuse

★ **Erie Canal Museum:** Learn about life on the Erie Canal and its economic significance to the region. The museum features an educational gallery, changing exhibits, children's activity centers, and a reproduction of a canal boat. Check out the slide show on the history of Syracuse.

★ **Milton J. Rubenstein Museum of Science & Technology:** Here you'll find interactive exhibits of science and technology. Be sure to check out the Bristol IMAX Omnitheater.

★ **New York State Fairgrounds:** If you visit Syracuse in August, head over to the New York State Fairgrounds for the annual New York State Fair. There you'll find the best New York has to offer in agriculture, entertainment, education, industry, technology, and much more. Want to know more? Visit www.nysfair.org.

★ **Syracuse University:** Take a tour of "The Hill," as the hilltop campus of Syracuse University is known. The famed Carrier Dome is where the Syracuse University Orange do battle in the Big East Conference in football, basketball, and lacrosse.

Ithaca

★ **Cornell University:** This Ivy League institution is both a private university and the federal land grant institution of New York. It boasts 14 colleges and schools, 4,000 courses, 70 undergraduate majors, and 93 graduate fields of study.

★ **Robert H. Treman State Park:** This popular tourist spot has rustic beauty with craggy gorges and winding trails bearing names such as Lucifer Falls and Devil's Kitchen.

Corning

★ **Corning Museum of Glass:** Dedicated to the art, history, science, and exhibition of glass, this museum is a place where everyone can join the fun. Watch glass being made on the Hot Glass Stage and browse the galleries to see what the world's finest glass artists have created, then roll up your sleeves, pick up a tool, and make your own masterpiece.

Corning Museum of Glass

CENTRAL LEATHER-STOCKING REGION

THINGS TO DO: Discover the history of baseball, take a swim, or enjoy an afternoon picnic.

Cooperstown

★ **Doubleday Field:** Enjoy a game at historic Doubleday Field, where the rules for baseball were first invented!

★ **Fenimore Art Museum:** Here you'll find one of the world's finest collections of American art, folk art, and Native American art.

★ **The Farmers' Museum:** Want to see what a 19th-century farm was really like? This museum features more than two dozen authentic buildings, as well as a children's barnyard.

SEE IT HERE!

NATIONAL BASEBALL HALL OF FAME

The newly renovated museum brings baseball's glorious history to life through interactive exhibits and emotional stories. The museum features the hallowed Hall of Fame Gallery, honoring the game's greatest players, as well as countless exhibits and statistical information for fans of all ages.

National Baseball Hall of Fame and Museum

Oneonta

★ **Greater Oneonta Historical Society:** As one of the largest historical groups in Central New York, the society works to preserve the heritage of the Greater Oneonta area. The society's holdings of more than 5,000 items consist of farm equipment, clothing, photographs, postcards, portraits, ephemera, and other historical regalia that pertain to the Upper Susquehanna region.

Adirondack Mountains

ADIRONDACKS— THOUSAND ISLANDS REGION

THINGS TO DO: Take a hike through the Adirondack Mountains, learn about the Iroquois Confederacy, or visit the home of famed writer Robert Louis Stevenson.

Adirondack

★ **Adirondack Museum:** The exhibits in this museum tell the story of the Adirondack region and its people. They include works of art, photographs, furniture, and boats.

★ **Great Camp Sagamore:** Located at Raquette Lake, the 27 buildings of the complex were once the wilderness retreat of the famed Vanderbilt family.

WOW

Lake Placid's bobsled run is often considered the most thrilling 43 seconds a human can spend.

★ **Adirondack Mountains:** These mountains are a haven for outdoor enthusiasts. Canoe, kayak, swim, and fish 3,000 ponds and lakes and 1,500 miles (2,414 km) of rivers.

Lake Placid

★ **Lake Placid:** Lake Placid boasts premier waterskiing, swimming, fishing, and hiking. Skiers, are you brave enough to attempt the biggest vertical drop in the East? You'll find that here, too.

Onchiota

★ **Six Nations Indian Museum:** You'll hear an elaborate storytelling of the Iroquois tribes of the Six Nations, view more than 3,000 artifacts and outdoor displays, and learn about the historic regional Iroquois Confederacy.

Saranac Lake

★ **Robert Louis Stevenson Memorial Cottage:** Visit the historic house museum of the author of *Treasure Island, Dr. Jekyll and Mr. Hyde,* and other timeless classics. Stevenson spent the winter of 1887–1888 writing *The Master of Ballantrae* at this cottage. It has been carefully preserved and offers a unique and intimate glimpse into the author's life.

CAPITAL SARATOGA REGION

THINGS TO DO: Tour the state capitol, learn about the Underground Railroad, or discover the history of dance.

Albany

★ **Albany Institute of History and Art:** Founded in 1791, this museum is dedicated to collecting, preserving, interpreting, and promoting interest in the history, art, and culture of Albany and the Upper Hudson River valley region.

★ **New York State Capitol:** A National Historic Landmark, it houses the governor's office and the state's legislative branch. See where decisions are made!

★ **New York State Museum:** Among its 12.5 million artifacts, this museum—one of the oldest research facilities in the nation—offers a look at the state's rich history.

★ **Underground Railroad History Project:** This nonprofit organization helps visitors discover the stories of the Underground Railroad, its conductors, and the people who made it to freedom. The group offers walking tours of sites throughout Albany, Troy, and Arbor Hill.

Saratoga

★ **National Museum of Dance and Hall of Fame:** This National Historic Landmark is devoted exclusively to American dance. The Hall of Fame, which was established in 1987, proudly honors individuals who have made pioneering contributions to the field of dance.

★ **National Museum of Racing and Hall of Fame:** The history of Thoroughbred horse racing is on display at this museum, including trophies, silks (the shirts worn by jockeys), and memorabilia. The Hall of Fame honors horses, jockeys, and trainers. There's even an interactive horse racing simulator.

Saratoga Racecourse

CATSKILLS— HUDSON VALLEY REGION

THINGS TO DO: Tour a military academy, visit a sculpture garden, or go for a scenic hike.

Catskill

★ **Catskill Fly Fishing Center and Museum:** This center teaches about the history of fly-fishing and helps preserve the environment that supports it. Check out the collection of angling equipment, art, and artifacts.

★ **Catskill State Park and Forest Preserve:** Spend a day or two hiking and camping in this scenic state park.

★ **Thomas Cole National Historic Site:** If you love landscape art, then drop by the Thomas Cole National Historic Site, former home of this famed Hudson River School artist.

West Point

★ **United States Military Academy at West Point:** You can take a guided tour of the facility, which dates back to 1802, and learn about military history at the West Point Museum.

Suspended at Storm King Art Center

Mountainville

★ **Storm King Art Center:** Check out this outdoor sculpture museum, where art and nature complement each other in a unique way. The work of renowned artists is displayed among 500 acres (202 ha) of scenic lawns.

Hyde Park

★ **Springwood:** This is the birthplace and home of Franklin Delano Roosevelt. Named a National Historic Site in 1946, it is the only place in the United States where a president was born, maintained a lifelong connection, and is buried.

★ **Vanderbilt Mansion:** Take a trip to a historic, elegant world by visiting the home of the Vanderbilts, once the most powerful family in the United States.

Poughkeepsie

★ **Vassar College:** Founded as a women's college in 1861, Vassar opened its doors to men in 1969 and has been coeducational ever since. Here you'll find the manuscripts and papers of writer Mary McCarthy, poet Robert Lowell, and woman suffrage activist Elizabeth Cady Stanton.

NEW YORK CITY—LONG ISLAND REGION

THINGS TO DO: Visit some of the finest art museums in the world, see a Broadway show, or climb to the top of the Empire State Building for a beautiful view of the city.

West Hills

★ **Walt Whitman Birthplace:** This historic site in rural Long Island honors poet Walt Whitman, who was born there in 1817.

Port Washington

★ **Sands Point Preserve:** Enjoy 216 acres (87 ha) of forests, meadows, shore cliffs, a freshwater pond, and nature trails.

Old Bethpage

★ **Old Bethpage Village Restoration:** This 100-acre (40-ha) outdoor, living museum lets visitors experience 19th-century life on Long Island. Visit beautiful homes, a one-room schoolhouse, shops, and an inn.

Cold Spring Harbor

★ **Cold Spring Harbor Whaling Museum:** This is a family activity center that celebrates Long Island's past. Learn about whales and find out about whale conservation.

Old Bethpage Village Restoration

Wantagh

★ **Jones Beach State Park:** Enjoy a day at this stunning beach, which offers 6.5 miles (10 km) of coastline, plus two swimming pools. The park is home to the Theodore Roosevelt Nature Center. You can also check out great concerts at the Jones Beach Theater.

New York City

★ **Statue of Liberty:** There are few symbols in the world better known than the Statue of Liberty. A gift to the American people from France, the statue was erected on Bedlow Island (now Liberty Island) in 1886. The statue stands 306 feet (93 m) tall and weights 450,000 pounds (204,000 kilograms).

★ **The Solomon R. Guggenheim Museum:** With its unique spiral design, this museum is nearly as interesting as its exhibits. The Guggenheim features artists and

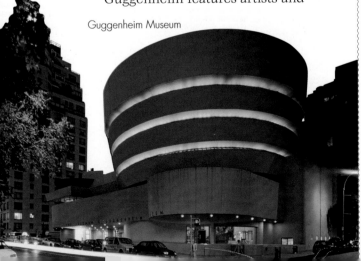

Guggenheim Museum

work both traditional and contemporary from all periods of art history. A truly remarkable collection!

★ **Ellis Island Immigration History Center:** When you visit this National Monument and museum, you'll gain extraordinary insight into the lives of more than 25 million immigrants from all over the world. They passed through this historic building on the way to a new life.

★ **The Metropolitan Museum of Art:** Nicknamed "the Met," it is home to millions of pieces of art and is considered one of the most important museums in the world.

★ **National Museum of the American Indian:** Come and visit one of the premier museums on Native American culture, literature, art, and history in the country!

SEE IT HERE!

CENTRAL PARK

How big is Central Park? Really big! In fact, it is 843 acres (341 ha), which is 6 percent of Manhattan's total area. If you walked all around the outside of the park, that's 6 miles (9.7 km). And if you visit the park, start counting: there are more than 26,000 trees, more than 9,000 benches, and 36 bridges and arches. The park was originally planned in 1858 by Frederick Law Olmstead and Calvert Vaux.

★ **Empire State Building Observatory:** You'll have a bird's-eye view of the city from atop the historic Empire State Building.

★ **Times Square Broadway District:** There's nothing like a Broadway show in the historic Theater District, and nowhere more exciting than Times Square. Times Square is the place the famous ball drops every New Year's Eve at midnight!

New York Aquarium

SEE IT HERE!

THE BRONX ZOO

Animal lovers should plan a full day at the Bronx Zoo, the largest city zoo in the United States. The Congo gorilla forest is an accurate replica of an African rain forest and home to a large group of gorillas living in a natural habitat. Visit the baboon reserve and observe the relationships between the mothers and their young. The Bronx Zoo is home to more than 4,000 animals belonging to 500 species. Many of these species are on the endangered species list (tigers, rhinos, and snow leopards, among others), and the zoo is a primary research facility for endangered species recovery programs.

Giraffe at the Bronx Zoo

★ **El Museo del Barrio:** This museum focuses on the art, literature, and culture of Spain, Portugal, the Philippines, and Latin America. Here you'll find works by Goya, El Greco, and Velasquez, as well as sculpture, cosmetic arts, textiles, and archaeological artifacts.

★ **New York Aquarium:** Located at Coney Island, this incredible place features more than 8,000 animals. You'll see penguins and beluga whales, sea lions and sharks, just to name a few.

★ **Yankee Stadium:** Head to the Bronx to the "House that Ruth built"—Yankee Stadium, and see the New York Yankees vie for another World Series championship.

WRITING PROJECTS

Check out these ideas for creating travel brochures and writing you-are-there editorials. Or learn about the state quarter and design your own.

118

ART PROJECTS 119

Act out interviews with famous people from the state, illustrate the state song, or create a great PowerPoint presentation.

TIMELINE

What happened when? This timeline highlights important events in the state's history—and shows what was happening throughout the United States at the same time.

122

GLOSSARY 125

Remember the Words to Know from the chapters in this book? They're all collected here.

FAST FACTS 126

Use this section to find fascinating facts about state symbols, land area and population statistics, weather, sports teams, and much more.

SCIENCE, TECHNOLOGY, ENGINEERING, & MATH PROJECTS

120

Make weather maps, graph population statistics, and research endangered species that live in the state.

PRIMARY VS. SECONDARY SOURCES

121

So what are primary and secondary sources? And what's the diff? This section explains all that and where you can find them.

BIOGRAPHICAL DICTIONARY

133

This at-a-glance guide highlights some of the state's most important and influential people. Visit this section and read about their contributions to the state, the country, and the world.

RESOURCES

Books and much more. Take a look at these additional sources for information about the state.

138

WRITING PROJECTS

Write a Memoir, Journal, or Editorial for Your School Newspaper!

Picture Yourself . . .

★ as a member of the Seneca, Onondaga, Oneida, Cayuga, or Mohawk tribe during the early days of New York. Think about what brought these tribes together to form the Iroquois League. Compose a letter to be circulated among members of all the groups proposing that the tribes join together to form the league. What reasons will you give?

   SEE: Chapter Two, pages 22–25.

★ as a reporter for your school newspaper, covering the first women's rights convention in Seneca Falls. Report on the event, and write your accounts of the various speeches you hear and people you meet. What are the major issues addressed during the convention? See if you can arrange an interview with one of the participants, perhaps Elizabeth Cady Stanton or Sojourner Truth.

   SEE: Chapter Four, pages 47–49.

Create an Election Brochure or Web Site!

★ Run for office! Throughout this book, you've read about some of the issues that concern New York today. As a candidate for governor of New York, create a campaign brochure or Web site.

★ Explain how you meet the qualifications to be governor of New York, and talk about the three or four major issues you'll focus on if you're elected.

   SEE: Chapter Seven, pages 85–87.

Research New York's State Quarter

From 1999 to 2008, the U.S. Mint introduced new quarters commemorating each of the 50 states in the order that they were admitted into the Union. Each state's quarter features a unique design on its reverse, or back.

GO TO: www.factsfornow.scholastic.com and enter the keywords **New York**. Look for the link to the New York quarter.

Research and write an essay explaining:

★ the significance of each image

★ who designed the quarter

★ who chose the final design.

Design your own New York state quarter. What images would you choose for the reverse?

★ Make a poster showing the New York quarter and label each image.

ART PROJECTS

Create a PowerPoint Presentation or Visitors' Guide
Welcome to New York!

New York's a great place to visit and to live! From its natural beauty to its bustling cities and historic sites, there's plenty to see and do. In your PowerPoint presentation or brochure, highlight 10 to 15 of New York's fascinating landmarks. Be sure to include:

★ a map of the state showing where these sites are located

★ photos, illustrations, Web links, natural history facts, geographic stats, climate and weather, plants and wildlife, recent discoveries.

SEE: Chapter Nine, pages 105–115.

Illustrate the Lyrics to the New York State Song
("I Love New York")

Use markers, paints, photos, collages, colored pencils, or computer graphics to illustrate the lyrics to "I Love New York," the state song! Turn your illustrations into a picture book, or scan them into a PowerPoint and add music!

SEE: The lyrics to "I Love New York" on page 128.

Conduct an Interview with a Famous New Yorker!

Gather up a pen, a notepad, a voice recorder, and a friend. Look online to see what you can find out about some of the famous people you have learned about in this book, including Lou Gehrig, Franklin Delano Roosevelt, Eleanor Roosevelt, Vera Wang, Jackie Robinson, Jennifer Lopez, and many more. Then, with a friend, write a script and perform an interview with that person on your voice recorder and present it to your class.

SEE: Chapters Six, Seven, and Eight, pages 76, 79–80, 91, and 98.

Statue of Liberty

SCIENCE, TECHNOLOGY, ENGINEERING, & MATH PROJECTS

Graph Population Statistics!

★ Compare population statistics (such as ethnic background, birth, death, and literacy rates) in New York counties or major cities.

★ In your graph or chart, look at population density, write sentences describing what the population statistics show; graph one set of population statistics and write a paragraph explaining what the graph reveals.

SEE: Chapter Six, pages 66–68.

Create a Weather Map of New York!

Use your knowledge of New York's geography to research and identify conditions that result in specific weather events. What is it about the geography of New York that makes it vulnerable to things such as blizzards? Create a weather map or poster that shows the weather patterns over the state. To accompany your map, explain the technology used to measure weather phenomena such as blizzards and provide data.

SEE: Chapter One, pages 16–17.

Track Endangered Species

Using your knowledge of New York's wildlife, research what animals and plants are endangered or threatened. Find out what the state is doing to protect these species. Chart known populations of the animals and plants, and report on changes in certain geographic areas.

SEE: Chapter One, page 19.

PRIMARY VS. SECONDARY SOURCES

What's the Diff?

Your teacher may require at least one or two primary sources and one or two secondary sources for your assignment. So, what's the difference between the two?

★ **Primary sources are original.** You are reading the actual words of someone's diary, journal, letter, autobiography or interview. Primary sources can also be photographs, maps, prints, cartoons, news/film footage, posters, first-person newspaper articles, drawings, musical scores, and recordings. By the way, when you conduct a survey, interview someone, shoot a video, or take photographs to include in a project, you are creating primary sources!

★ **Secondary sources are what you find in encyclopedias, textbooks, articles, biographies, and almanacs.** These are written by a person or group of people who tell about something that happened to someone else. Secondary sources also recount what another person said or did. This book is an example of a secondary source.

Now that you know what primary sources are—where can you find them?

★ **Your school or local library:** Check the library catalog for collections of original writings, government documents, musical scores, and so on. Some of this material may be stored on microfilm.

★ **Historical societies:** These organizations keep historical documents, photographs, and other materials. Staff members can help you find what you are looking for. History museums are also great places to see primary sources firsthand.

★ **The Internet:** There are lots of sites that have primary sources you can download and use in a project or assignment.

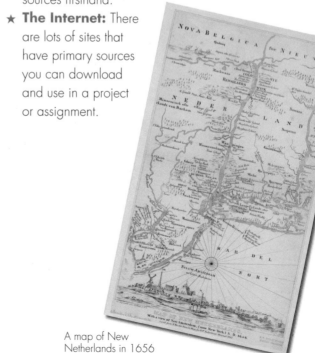

A map of New Netherlands in 1656

TIMELINE

★ ★ ★

U.S. Events New York Events

1524
Giovanni da Verrazano sails along America's northeast coast.

1565
Spanish admiral Pedro Menéndez de Avilés founds St. Augustine, Florida, the oldest continuously occupied European settlement in the continental United States.

1570
The Iroquois League is formed as oldest American democracy.

1600

1607
The first permanent English settlement in North America is established at Jamestown.

1609
Henry Hudson's *Half Moon* sails into New York Bay.

1620
Pilgrims found Plymouth Colony, the second permanent English settlement.

1624
The Dutch West India Company settles New Netherlands colony.

1626
Peter Minuet arrives as governor and purchases Manhattan Island for $24 in trinkets from the Canarsee Indians; the first 11 enslaved African men arrive.

1640
New Amsterdam becomes the first self-governing colony.

1660
New Amsterdam becomes North America's leading slave port.

Slave market

1664
Duke of York captures New Amsterdam and New Netherlands.

1682
René-Robert Cavelier, Sieur de La Salle, claims more than 1 million square miles (2.6 million sq km) of territory in the Mississippi River basin for France, naming it Louisiana.

U.S. Events | 1700 | New York Events

1714
The Iroquois League admits the Tuscarora as the sixth member.

1776
Thirteen American colonies declare their independence from Britain, marking the beginning of the Revolutionary War.

1777
The Battle of Saratoga, a major victory for the Revolution, is fought.

1787
The U.S. Constitution is written.

1785–90
New York serves as the first capital of the United States.

1788
New York becomes the 11th state.

1789
George Washington is inaugurated as president in New York City.

New York Stock Exchange

1792
The New York Stock Exchange is created.

1797
Albany becomes the capitol of New York.

1803 | 1800
The Louisiana Purchase almost doubles the size of the United States.

1825
The Erie Canal unites all of New York with the Great Lakes states.

1827
Slavery is abolished in New York.

1830
The Indian Removal Act forces eastern Native American groups to relocate west of the Mississippi River.

1848
Women gather in Seneca Falls for the first women's rights convention.

1861–65
The American Civil War is fought between the Northern Union and the Southern Confederacy; it ends with the surrender of the Confederate army, led by General Robert E. Lee.

1863
The New York City Draft Riots mark the worst urban upheaval in U.S. history.

1883
The Brooklyn Bridge is completed.

U.S. Events

1886
Apache leader Geronimo surrenders to the U.S. Army, ending the last major Native American rebellion against the expansion of the United States into the West.

1917–18
The United States engages in World War I.

1920
The Nineteenth Amendment to the U.S. Constitution grants women the right to vote.

1929
The stock market crashes, plunging the United States deeper into the Great Depression.

1941–45
The United States engages in World War II.

1964–73
The United States engages in the Vietnam War.

1991
The United States engages in the Persian Gulf War.

2001
Terrorists hijack four U.S. aircraft and crash them, killing thousands.

2003
The United States and coalition forces invade Iraq.

New York Events

1886
The Statue of Liberty is unveiled in New York Harbor.

1900

1902
Manhattan's Flatiron Building opens for business.

1917
New York women gain the right to vote.

1920s
The Harlem Renaissance celebrates black talent and pride.

1931
The Empire State Building is completed.

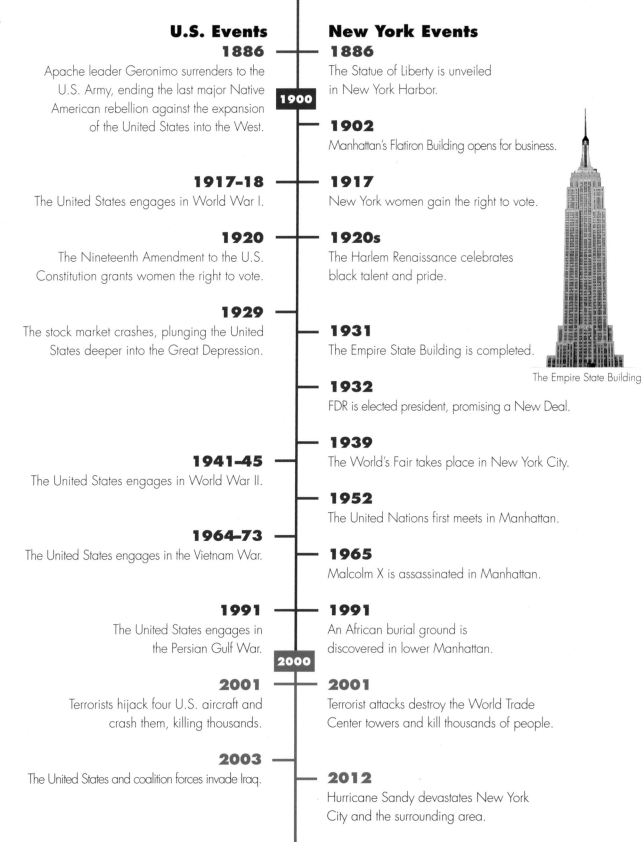

The Empire State Building

1932
FDR is elected president, promising a New Deal.

1939
The World's Fair takes place in New York City.

1952
The United Nations first meets in Manhattan.

1965
Malcolm X is assassinated in Manhattan.

1991
An African burial ground is discovered in lower Manhattan.

2000

2001
Terrorist attacks destroy the World Trade Center towers and kill thousands of people.

2012
Hurricane Sandy devastates New York City and the surrounding area.

GLOSSARY

abolitionists people who were opposed to slavery and worked to end it

acid rain pollution that falls to the earth in the form of rain

algae plant or plantlike organisms that live in water

aqueducts structures for carrying large amounts of flowing water

civil rights basic rights that are guaranteed to all people under the U.S. Constitution

colony a community settled in a new land but with ties to another government

confederation an association of groups that come together with common goals

emancipation the act of freeing slaves from bondage

fugitives people who are trying to flee or escape

hazardous waste chemical materials that are harmful to the environment

impeachment the act of charging a political official with misconduct while in office, sometimes resulting in removal from office

indentured servants people who sign agreements to work for a given amount of time; they are not paid, but receive room and board

inflation a condition in which the prices of goods increase faster than wages

locks enclosures in canals with gates on each end that help boats pass from level to level

longhouse a long building used by an entire Native American community

metropolitan relating to a city and its surroundings

persecution mistreatment of people because of their beliefs

precipitation all water that falls to earth, including rain, sleet, hail, snow, dew, fog, or mist

probation a time during which a person convicted of a crime is evaluated

sachems representatives of Native American clans

shaman a Native American spiritual leader

stock a monetary investment in a company

strike an organized refusal to work, usually as a sign of protest about working conditions

Utopian describing a society that is ideal and perfect

FAST FACTS

★ ★ ★

State Symbols

Statehood date	July 26, 1788, the 11th state
Origin of state name	Named for the Duke of York
State capital	Albany
State nickname	Empire State
State motto	"Excelsior" ("Ever Upward")
State bird	Bluebird
State flower	Rose
State fish	Brook trout
State song	"I Love New York" (See page 128 for lyrics)
State tree	Sugar maple
State fruit	Apple
State animal	Beaver
State gem	Wine-red garnet
State fossil	*Eurypterus remipes* (sea scorpion)
State muffin	Apple muffin
State fair	Syracuse (late August–early September)

State seal

Geography

Total area; rank	54,556 square miles (141,300 sq km); 27th
Land; rank	47,214 square miles (122,284 sq km); 30th
Water; rank	7,342 square miles (19,016 sq km); 7th
Inland water; rank	1,895 square miles (4,908 sq km); 10th
Coastal water; rank	981 square miles (2,541 sq km); 7th
Great Lakes; rank	3,988 square miles (10,329 sq km); 3rd
Territorial water; rank	479 square miles (1,241 sq km); 14th
Geographic center	Madison County, 12 miles (19 km) south of Oneida and 26 miles (42 km) southwest of Utica
Latitude	40° 29' 40" N to 45° 0' 42" N
Longitude	71° 47' 25" W to 79° 45' 54" W
Highest point	Mount Marcy, 5,344 feet (1,629 m)
Lowest point	Sea level at the Atlantic Ocean
Largest city	New York City
Number of counties	62
Longest river	Hudson River, 306 miles (492 km)

Population

Population; rank (2010 census):	19,378,102; 3rd
Density (2010 census):	411 persons per square mile (159 per sq km)
Population distribution (2010 census):	88% urban, 12% rural
Race (2010 census):	White persons: 58.3%
	Black persons: 14.4%
	Asian persons: 7.3%
	American Indian and Alaska Native persons: 0.3%
	Persons reporting two or more races: 1.7%
	Hispanic or Latino persons: 17.6%
	People of some other race: 0.4%

Weather

Record high temperature	108°F (42°C) at Troy on July 22, 1926
Record low temperature	−52°F (−47°C) at Old Forge on February 18, 1979
Average July temperature, New York City	77°F (25°C)
Average January temperature, New York City	33°F (−1°C)
Average annual precipitation, New York City	45 inches (114 cm)

State flag

Digging out after an
Albany snowstorm

STATE SONG

★ ★ ★

"I Love New York"

Words and music by Steve Karmen

The "I ♥ NY" slogan and logo was developed to promote tourism in New York State. Created by graphic artist Milton Glaser, it was first used in 1977. The song "I Love New York" was donated by Steve Karmen, who composed scores of stick-in-your-head jingles for products such as Hershey's chocolate bars.

I love New York,
I love New York,
I love New York.
    There isn't another like it
No matter where you go.
And nobody can compare it.
It's win and place and show.
New York is special.
New York is diff'rent 'cause there's
no place else on earth quite like
New York and that's why
    I love New York,
I love New York,
I love New York.

NATURAL AREAS AND HISTORIC SITES

National Historic Sites

Eleanor Roosevelt National Historic Site (Hyde Park) is the first lady's home, Val-Kill.

Sagamore Hill National Historic Site is the home of Theodore Roosevelt, where he lived from 1886 to 1919.

Theodore Roosevelt Inaugural National Historic Site preserves the Ansley Wilcox House in Buffalo where the vice president took the oath of office upon the assassination of President William McKinley.

Vanderbilt Mansion National Historic Site is a stately mansion along the Hudson River.

National Historical Parks

Saratoga National Historical Park is the site of an important American Revolution battle.

Women's Rights National Historical Park memorializes the place of the important early meetings for equal rights for women in the United States.

National Monuments

Statue of Liberty National Monument is home to the massive statue that has become a worldwide symbol of freedom.

Ellis Island National Monument offers insight into the lives of the more than 25 million immigrants who passed through here.

National Scenic and Recreation River

Upper Delaware National Scenic and Recreation River is 73 miles (117 km) of free-flowing river along the New York and Pennsylvania border.

State Parks and Forests

New York has 179 state parks. *Adirondack Park and Forest Preserve* is the largest.

Other Sites Maintained by the National Park Service

Two national scenic trails cross parts of New York. The state is also home to a national seashore and national heritage corridor.

SPORTS TEAMS

★ ★ ★

NCAA Teams (Division I)

Albany University *Great Danes*
Canisius College *Golden Griffins*
Colgate University *Red Raiders*
Columbia University *Lions*
Cornell University *Big Red*
Fordham University *Rams*
Hofstra University *Pride*
Iona College *Gaels*
Long Island University *Blackbirds*
Manhattan College *Jaspers*
Marist College *Red Foxes*

Niagara University *Purple Eagles*
Siena College *Saints*
State University of New York–Binghamton *Bearcats*
State University of New York–Buffalo *Bulls*
State University of New York–Stony Brook *Seawolves*
St. Bonaventure University *Bonnies*
St. Francis College *Terriers*
St. John's University *Red Storm*
Syracuse University *Orange*
U.S. Military Academy at West Point *Black Knights*
Wagner College *Seahawks*

PROFESSIONAL SPORTS TEAMS

★ ★ ★

Major League Baseball
New York *Mets*
New York *Yankees*

National Basketball Association
New York *Knickerbockers*

National Football League
Buffalo *Bills*
New York *Giants*
New York *Jets*

National Hockey League
New York *Rangers*
Buffalo *Sabres*
New York *Islanders*

Women's National Basketball Association
New York *Liberty*

Major League Soccer
New York *Red Bulls*

CULTURAL INSTITUTIONS

★ ★ ★

Libraries

Columbia University Library (New York City) and *Cornell University Library* (Ithaca) are among the largest collections in the world.

Franklin D. Roosevelt Library (Hyde Park) is the official library for the 32nd president.

The *New York Public Library* is the largest public library in the nation.

The *Schomburg Center for Research in Black Culture* is part of the New York Public Library and is devoted to African American history.

Museums

Corning Museum of Glass (Corning) houses 45,000 objects made of glass spanning 3,500 years.

The *Erie Canal Museum* (Syracuse) chronicles the history of the canal.

The *National Baseball Hall of Fame and Museum* (Cooperstown) offers the history of this sport.

The *New York State Museum* (Albany) takes a look at the state's heritage.

The *Metropolitan Museum of Art* (New York City) is home to more than 3.3 million international treasures.

The *Museum of Modern Art* (New York City) has been home to one of the world's greatest art collections since its founding in 1929.

Performing Arts

The *New York Philharmonic* (New York City) is the oldest symphony orchestra in the nation and one of the oldest in the world.

The *New York City Ballet* is widely considered to be one of the greatest dance companies in the world.

Universities and Colleges

In 2011, New York had 45 public and 182 private institutions of higher learning.

ANNUAL EVENTS

January–March

Winterfest in Syracuse (mid-February)

Westminster Kennel Club Dog Show in New York City (February)

Winter Carnival in Saranac Lake (February)

St. Patrick's Day Parade in New York City (March)

April–June

Schoharie County Maple Festival in Jefferson (April)

Hudson River Whitewater Derby in North Creek (May)

National Lake Trout Derby on Seneca Lake near Geneva (May)

Rochester Lilac Festival in Rochester (May)

Dressage at Saratoga in Saratoga (Memorial Day weekend)

Empire State Regatta in Albany (June)

Belmont Stakes Horse Race on Long Island (early June)

July–September

Friendship Festival in Buffalo (July)

National Baseball Hall of Fame Induction Ceremony in Cooperstown (late July or early August)

German Alps Festival in Hunter, near Tannersville (August)

Central New York Scottish Games in Liverpool (August)

Adirondack Balloon Festival in Glens Falls (September)

October–December

Oyster Festival in Oyster Bay, Long Island (October)

New York Marathon in New York City (November)

Thanksgiving Day Parade in New York City (November)

Annual Snowbird Soaring Regatta at Elmira (late November)

Winter Festival of Lights in Niagara Falls (Thanksgiving to early January)

Rockefeller Center Tree Lighting Ceremony in New York City (December)

BIOGRAPHICAL DICTIONARY

Kareem Abdul-Jabbar

Kareem Abdul-Jabbar (1947–) was born in Harlem and loved playing basketball there. He went on to be an NBA starter for the Milwaukee Bucks and the Los Angeles Lakers.

Susan B. Anthony See page 48.

John Jacob Astor (1763–1848) was a self-made millionaire who earned his money through the fur trade. Born in Germany, he immigrated to the United States at age 20. He owned large blocks of real estate in Manhattan.

James Baldwin (1924–1987), was a writer born in Harlem. *Go Tell It on the Mountain*, although a novel, tells about his youth. Other well-known works include *Notes of a Native Son* and *Nobody Knows My Name*.

Jean-Michel Basquiat (1960–1988) was an artist who was first noticed by the artistic world through his graffiti on the streets and subways of New York.

L. Frank Baum (1856–1919) was the author of *The Wonderful Wizard of Oz* and other novels. He was born in Chittenango.

Romare Bearden (1911–1988) was a painter and creator of collages, contributing to the cubist, abstract, and social realist art movements. He was born in Charlotte, North Carolina, but spent his career in New York.

Elizabeth Blackwell (1821–1910) was the first woman to earn a medical degree in the United States. She earned hers from Geneva Medical College in 1849.

Mel Brooks (1926–) was born in Brooklyn as Melvin Kaminsky. He started his professional career as a stand-up comic and went on to be an award-winning film director and producer.

Joseph Bruchac See page 75.

Benjamin Cardozo (1870–1938) served on the U.S. Supreme Court from 1932 until his death. He was the second person of the Jewish faith to be appointed to the court, after Louis Brandeis.

Mariah Carey (1970–) is a pop and R & B singer, songwriter, and music producer. Among the best-selling female artists of all time, she was born on Long Island.

Shirley Chisholm (1924–2005) was a New York City schoolteacher who was born in Brooklyn. She became the first African American woman elected to Congress, serving from 1969 to 1982.

Mariah Carey

Grover Cleveland See page 91.

George Clinton See page 87.

Thomas Cole (1801–1848) was a landscape artist who is known as the founder of the Hudson River School art movement. Born in England, he moved to New York City as a young man.

Verplanck Colvin (1847–1920) was an environmentalist. He helped create the Adirondack Forest Preserve in 1885.

James Fenimore Cooper (1789–1851) was a writer who lived in what is now Cooperstown. He is best remembered for a series of books called the Leatherstocking Tales.

Aaron Copland (1900–1990) was one of America's leading composers, whose best-known works include *Rodeo, Appalachian Spring*, and *A Lincoln Portrait*. He was born in Brooklyn.

Countee Cullen (1903–1946) was a poet of the Harlem Renaissance. *The Black Christ* and *One Way to Heaven* are among his best-known works. He was adopted and raised in Harlem.

Mario Cuomo (1932–) was the governor of New York State from 1983 to 1994, known for his liberal political views. He is the father of Andrew Cuomo, who was elected the state's governor in 2010.

Claire Danes (1979–) is an actor whose films include *The Family Stone* and *Shopgirl* as well as the TV series *Homeland*. She was born in New York City.

Claire Danes

David Dinkins (1927–) was elected as the first African American mayor of New York City in 1989. He was born in Trenton, New Jersey.

George Eastman (1854–1932) encouraged popular interest in photography through his development of the Kodak camera. He was born in Waterville.

Edward "Duke" Ellington (1899–1974) was one of the premier bandleaders of the Harlem Renaissance. Born in Washington, D.C., he moved to New York in 1923.

Millard Fillmore See page 91.

Marcus Garvey (1887–1940) was born in Jamaica. He came to New York in the 1920s to generate interest in the black nationalist movement.

Lou Gehrig (1903–1941) was a legendary baseball player for the New York Yankees. He was born in New York City.

Sarah Michelle Gellar (1977–) is an actor known for her roles in TV's *Buffy the Vampire Slayer* and films such as *Scooby-Doo* and *I Know What You Did Last Summer*. She was born in New York City.

George Gershwin (1898–1937) was a popular composer known for *Rhapsody in Blue* and the opera *Porgy and Bess*. He was born in Brooklyn.

Rudolph Giuliani (1944–) was the mayor of New York for many years. When the World Trade Center was attacked on September 11, 2001, he led the city through the crisis. He was born in New York City.

Cuba Gooding Jr. (1968–) is an Academy Award–winning actor who has starred in films such as *Snow Dogs* and *Pearl Harbor*. He was born in the Bronx.

David Dinkins

Oscar Hammerstein II (1895–1960) was a composer and a theater director of musicals best known for the many hit songs he wrote that appeared in Broadway shows. Musicals for which he composed include *The Sound of Music, The King and I, Oklahoma!*, and *South Pacific.*

Rabbi Abraham Joshua Heschel (1907–1972) escaped Nazi-occupied Europe and found refuge in the United States. He taught at New York City's Jewish Theological Seminary and was an activist for social reform. In 1963, he marched with Martin Luther King Jr. in a historic protest for civil rights.

Julia Ward Howe (1819–1910) wrote the lyrics to "The Battle Hymn of the Republic," a march made popular during the Civil War. She was born in New York City.

Langston Hughes (1902–1967) was a poet who gained recognition during the Harlem Renaissance. He was born in Missouri, raised in Kansas, and later moved to New York City.

Washington Irving (1783–1859) wrote many short stories and tales of New York's Dutch colonial days, including *Rip Van Winkle* and *The Legend of Sleepy Hollow*. He was born in New York City.

Henry James (1843–1916) wrote about New York society in his novel *Washington Square*. Other famous novels include *The Turn of the Screw* and *The Golden Bowl*. He was born in New York City.

Billy Joel (1949–) is a singer and composer who hit the top of the music charts with albums such as *Piano Man* and *River of Dreams*. Born in the Bronx, he often sings about his home state.

Scarlett Johansson (1984–) is an actress and singer whose films, include *The Avengers, Iron Man II, Lost in Translation*, and *Ghost World*. She has performed in plays in New York and has released two record albums. She was born in New York City.

Alicia Keys (1980–) is a Grammy Award–winning pop and R & B singer and songwriter. She was born in New York City.

Lady Gaga (Stefani Joanne Angelina Germanotta) (1986–) is a singer and songwriter whose musical style and sense of fashion have become legendary. With more than 23 million albums sold worldwide and numerous Grammy Awards, she is one of the 21st century's most popular performers. She grew up in New York City.

Alicia Keys

Fiorello LaGuardia See page 60.

Spike Lee (1957–) is a film director, actor, writer, and producer. Born in Atlanta, he moved to Brooklyn as a child. He also is a film teacher at New York University.

Madeleine L'Engle (1918–2007) is a writer of children's books such as the Newbery Award–winning *A Wrinkle in Time*. She was born in New York City.

Madeleine L'Engle

Yo-Yo Ma See page 77.

Malcolm X See page 62.

Claude McKay (1890–1948) was a writer during the Harlem Renaissance who was born in Jamaica. Some of his works include *Home to Harlem* and *A Long Way Home*.

Jacqueline Kennedy Onassis (1929–1994) was the wife of John F. Kennedy and first lady of the United States during his presidency from 1961 until his death in 1963. She later worked as an editor and also supported numerous programs that worked to preserve and protect America's cultural heritage. She grew up in New York City.

Robert Oppenheimer (1904–1967), born in New York City, was a scientist and professor of physics at the University of California. He is often called the "father of the atomic bomb" for his role in the World War II project that developed the first nuclear weapons.

Jackson Pollock (1912–1956) was a painter in the abstract expressionist movement. He was born in Wyoming but lived on Long Island for much of his life.

Colin Powell (1937–) was a four-star general in the U.S. Army, and the secretary of state from 2001 to 2005, the first African American to hold that position. Powell served in the Vietnam War (1955–1975) and was chairman of the Joint Chiefs of Staff, leading the planning of Operation Desert Storm in 1991.

Norman Rockwell (1894–1978) was a popular artist who depicted the lives of average Americans in his covers for the *Saturday Evening Post*. He was born in New York City.

John (1806–1869), **Washington (1837–1926)**, and **Emily Roebling (1843–1903)** played key roles in the building of the Brooklyn Bridge.

Eleanor Roosevelt See page 91.

Franklin D. Roosevelt See page 91.

Theodore Roosevelt See page 91.

David Ruggles See page 46.

Carl Sagan (1934–1996), born in New York City, was an astronomer and author. His 13-part TV series, *Cosmos: A Personal Voyage*, was shown in more than 60 countries and introduced more than 500 million viewers to the science of astronomy.

Sagoyewatha/Red Jacket (1758?–1830) was a Seneca chief who fought alongside the British during the Revolutionary War and against the British during the War of 1812.

Jonas Salk (1914–1995) was a doctor who worked with the influenza virus, but is best known for the oral vaccine for polio. He was born in New York City.

Adam Sandler (1966–) is a comedian who got his start on *Saturday Night Live*. Born in Brooklyn, he is known for his film roles in *50 First Dates* and *The Wedding Singer*.

Adam Sandler

Arturo Schomburg

Augusta Savage (1892–1962) was a sculptor who was active during the Harlem Renaissance. Born in Florida, she later made her home in New York City.

Arturo Schomburg (1874–1938) was a historian, writer, and activist. His collection of art, books, manuscripts, and other artifacts from black history are now part of the New York Public Library. Born in Puerto Rico, he moved to New York City as a young man.

Pete Seeger (1919–) is a singer and activist. Born in New York City, he lives in Fishkill.

Rod Serling (1924–1975) was a screenwriter who is best remembered for the TV show *The Twilight Zone*. He was born in Syracuse and grew up in Binghamton.

Judith Sheindlin (1942–), better known as TV's Judge Judy, is a lawyer, author, and media celebrity. Before her TV success, she was a prosecutor in the New York City courts system and later a judge in the city's criminal courts.

Joanne Shenandoah See page 26.

Elizabeth Cady Stanton (1815–1902) was a leader in the women's rights movement. She was born in Johnstown.

Barbra Streisand (1942–) is a singer, actor, and director who won an Academy Award for her role in *Funny Girl*. Other Streisand films include *Hello, Dolly!*, *The Way We Were*, and *Yentl*. She was born in Brooklyn.

Peter Stuyvesant (c. 1612–1672) served as the last leader of the Dutch colony of New Amsterdam, which was renamed New York. He remained in the region until his death.

Thayendanegea/Joseph Brant (1743–1807) was a Mohawk chief who fought alongside the British during the American Revolutionary War.

Sojourner Truth See page 47.

Martin Van Buren See page 91.

Giovanni da Verrazano See page 30.

A'Lelia Walker (1885–1931) was the daughter of Madam C. J. Walker. She hosted readings and other cultural events during the Harlem Renaissance.

Madam C. J. Walker (1867–1919) was an inventor and businessperson. Born in Louisiana, she moved to New York City, where she created and sold Madam Walker's Wonderful Hair Grower.

Mary Edwards Walker (1832–1919) was born in Oswego to a family of abolitionists. She was an activist for women's rights and served as an assistant surgeon during the Civil War.

Fats Waller (1904–1943) was a singer, jazz pianist, and composer from New York City whose best-known compositions, "Ain't Misbehavin'" and "Honeysuckle Rose," have been recorded by many performers. He was honored with a Grammy Lifetime Achievement Award in 1993.

Vera Wang See page 98.

Walt Whitman (1819–1892) was a poet whose best-known works include *Leaves of Grass*, "O Captain! My Captain!" and "When Lilacs Last in the Dooryard Bloom'd." He was born in West Hills.

RESOURCES

BOOKS

Nonfiction

Dolbear, Emily J., and Peter Benoit. *The Iroquois*. New York: Children's Press, 2011.

Kendall, Martha E. *The Erie Canal*. Washington, D.C.: National Geographic, 2008.

Mann, Elizabeth. *Statue of Liberty: A Tale of Two Countries*. New York: Mikaya Press, 2011.

Todd, Anne M. *Susan B. Anthony: Activist*. New York: Chelsea House, 2009.

Young, Jeff C. *Henry Hudson: Discoverer of the Hudson River*. Berkeley Heights, N.J.: Enslow Publishers, 2009.

Fiction

Bruchac, Joseph. *Hidden Roots*. New York: Scholastic, 2006.

Konigsburg, E. L. *From the Mixed-Up Files of Mrs. Basil E. Frankweiler*. New York: Yearling, 1977.

Selden, George. *The Cricket in Times Square*. New York: Yearling, 1970.

Sterman, Betsy. *Saratoga Secret*. New York: Dial, 1998.

White, E. B. *Stuart Little*. New York: HarperTrophy, 1974.

Visit this Scholastic Web site for more information on New York:
www.factsfornow.scholastic.com
Enter the keywords **New York**

INDEX

★ ★ ★

AUTHOR'S TIPS AND SOURCE NOTES

★　★　★

My biggest challenge in writing this book was to cut down the material. While there are dozens of excellent books on New York history, *The Empire State: A History of New York*, edited by Milton M. Klein, proved most helpful. A tip on researching such a popular topic: narrow your search. An Internet search of the term "New York" returns more hits than anyone could go through. Even "New York sports" finds thousands of available options. Focus in on just what you want to know—"New York professional sports teams." Just be sure to use reputable Web sites. Look for those that are run by government agencies or educational organizations (and end with "gov" and "edu").

Photographs ©: age fotostock: 84 (Dennis MacDonald), 103 bottom (Jim Toomey); Alamy Images: 14, 48 top (Andre Jenny), 69 (David Grossman), 94, 95 left (Dennis Hallinan), 16 (Ellen McKnight), 88 (Frances M. Roberts), 110 (James Schwabel), 21 bottom left (North Wind Picture Archives), 20 top, 21 left (Stock Montage, Inc.); AP Images: 99 right (Charles Sykes), 79 (Damen Jackson via Triple Play New Media), 78 (David Drapkin), 5 top right, 55 bottom, 62 (Eddie Adams), 76 top (Express Newspapers), 47 (Library of Congress), 4 bottom, 81 left (Lionel Cironneau), 26 (Michael Okoniewski), 109, 127 bottom (Mike Groll), 111 (Reid Burchell), 82, 83 left (Tim Roske); Art Resource, NY: 41 bottom right, 50 (New York Public Library), 5 top center, 46 bottom (Schomburg Center/NYPL); Buddy Mays/Travel Stock: 4 center left, 9 top, 19; Chautauqua Institute/Bruce Fox: 107; Corbis Images: 54 bottom, 124 (Alan Schein Photography), 70 (Andrew Lichtenstein), 112 (ART on FILE), 21 top, 27, 61, 80, 87 (Bettmann), 133 left (Bonnie Schiffman), 136 (Frank Trapper), 106 (Free Agents Limited), 63 (Geray Sweeney), 5 top left, 41 top, 44 (Lewis Wickes Hine/Bettmann), 29 top, 34, 122 (Museum of the City of New York), 74 (Richard Schulman), 40 top, 41 left, 58, 137; Corning Museum of Glass: 108; Digital Railroad/Rick Shupper/Ambient Images: 65 top, 66, 115 bottom; Dreamstime: 64, 65 (Andykazie), 8, 9 left (Rabbit75); Envision Stock Photography Inc./Steven Needham: 72; Getty Images: 135 top (Brad Barket), 81 right (Dave Hogan/NBC/NBCU Photo Bank), 115 top (Dave King), 98 (Donna Ward), 95 top, 97 (Mario Tama), 133 right, 134 left (Peter Kramer); Inmagine: 83 top, 92, 127 top; iStockphoto: 116 top right, 117, 130 right (David Freund), 116 bottom, 130 left (Geoffrey Black), 29 bottom left, 123 right (Hannamaria Photography), 103 top (Henry Chaplin), 5 bottom, 41 bottom left, 52, 119 (Natalie Helbert), 128 (Vladislav Lebedinski); Jennifer Keane/Lucence Photographic: 99 left; Library of Congress: 53 (Currier & Ives), 60 (Fred Palumbo), 48 bottom (Mrs. L. Condon); Nativestock. com/Marilyn "Angel" Wynn: 4 center, 21 bottom right; New York Public Library Picture Collection/Adriaen van der Donck/Mid-Manhattan Library Picture Collection: 121; North Wind Picture Archives: 4 center right, 28 bottom, 30; Periodyssey/Richard Samuel West Collection: 46 top; PictureHistory.com: 40 bottom right, 40 bottom left, 42, 123 left; Redux Pictures/Richard Perry/The New York Times Co: 134 right; ShutterStock, Inc./Alex Star: 73; SODA: 135 bottom; Superstock, Inc.: 114 (age fotostock), 4 top, 20 bottom (Christie's Images), 29 bottom right; The Granger Collection, New York: 25, 38, 54 top, 55 top, 55 left, 56; The Image Works: 91 (Ann Ronan Picture Library/HIP), 10 (Joseph Sohm), 76 bottom, 113 (Lee Snider), 28 top (Mary Evans Picture Library), 75 (Michael Greenlar), 12 (Monika Graff), 29 left (Museum of the City of New York), 77 (Nina Large/ArenaPAL/Topham); US Mint: 116 top left, 118; Vector-Images.com: 93, 126.

Maps by Map Hero, Inc.